The Best of

John Axe

Article and Book Reprints 1976 to 1987

Edited by Virginia Ann Heyerdahl

Published by   Hobby House Press   Cumberland Maryland 21502

DEDICATION

Dedicated to the Memory of
C. Kenneth Clark, Jr.
Who for a quarter of a century always advised me well.

TABLE OF CONTENTS

INTRODUCTION

The dolls shown in this book are among my favorites. I have a great many favorites and it would be easier to tell which dolls that I do not like. All dolls are fun to collect and the main reason is probably because they are small replicas of the most fascinating things there are — real people. Many of the dolls shown in this book appealed to me so much that they became the subjects of my research books and monographs.

I first began to research and write about dolls in the early 1970s. I had liked and collected dolls most of my life. The first ones that I deliberately collected were antique bisque dolls because I liked old dolls and they were affordable at the time. In the early 1960s, a nice bisque or china doll cost about $20, and I found them mostly at antique shows. Later I began to appreciate composition and hard plastic dolls, which were even more reasonable and could be purchased from doll dealers. An all-original Madame Alexander hard plastic doll from the 1950s cost about $15 in the early 1970s while all-original composition dolls from the 1930s were about $25. We all know that even then those dolls were bargains when we note their values today.

Once I began collecting more earnestly, I soon amassed a large collection of dolls that I liked. Like most collectors of something worth collecting, I wanted to know the history and background of the dolls. In the early 1970s there was very little information available about the dolls from the 1930s through the 1960s, other than a few books which showed photographs of the dolls and described them. I wanted to know about the companies which made them, the people who designed them and why they were made.

I set out to investigate the backgrounds of the dolls and the causes that stimulated their manufacture. I had heard of Toni Home Permanents, which inspired the manufacture of the *Toni*® dolls, but I knew nothing about the company or the procedures that transpired to make dolls that capitalized on the popularity of home permanents. I had never heard of Harriet Hubbard Ayer, or the cosmetic company which lent its name to the doll which I could identify by name. Other dolls, like the composition *Patsy*, were already the subject of several small books, but many of the details I wanted to know about the various dolls developed from *Patsy* were missing in these books, so I began to investigate their backgrounds, learning, among other things, that they too reflected the tastes and traditions of the times in which they were produced. At the time I wrote **Collectible Black Dolls**, almost nothing existed in print about these highly-prized collectibles.

Among the various dolls told about in this book are articles on several celebrity dolls — dolls made in the image of a famous person, or bearing the name of a famous person and capturing their persona with costumes or accessories. I had to know the history and the background of the celebrity and discover what it was about the person that inspired doll production. Mostly it was their fame, which by the time I had purchased the dolls, for example Anne Shirley, had passed as so much time had gone by. These dolls are more exciting when the story of the real person is known also.

The first book I researched and wrote was **The Co[llectible Dionne Quintuplets]**. At the time I began collec[t]ing the dolls, I had heard of the famous babies fro[m] Canada who were all identical, but I knew very littl[e] about the details of their miraculous births and th[e] events of their lives. I soon learned how tremendousl[y] popular the Dionne Quintuplets were in the 1930s an[d] how marketable their images were for all sorts of con[sumer goods and advertisement endorsements. It [i]s also fun to complement a doll collection with all th[e] auxiliary collectibles that relate to the dolls, such as D[i]onne Quintuplet paper dolls, spoons, dishes and toys[,] and advertising materials such as calendars and pape[r] fans.

I am also especially fond of character dolls that de[r]ived from popular images in fiction, the movies or fro[m] radio and television. I knew of Charlie McCarthy and could readily identify him in doll form but I wanted t[o] investigate the story behind the creation of the characte[r] and clear up some misconceptions about the variou[s] *Charlie McCarthy* dolls and other similar type ventriloqu[i]st dolls from the late 1930s. I remembered Howd[y] Doody very well from when I was young, but I neve[r] knew about all the collectibles, especially dolls, that ha[d] been available when he was first popular in the earl[y] 1950s. As an adult, I discovered him all over again.

Of all dolls, toys and collectibles, my most favorite [of] all is Pinocchio, based on the image created by Wa[lt] Disney for the 1940 full-length film. The first toy I ca[n] remember receiving was a *Pinocchio* doll, for my first [or] second Christmas. Happy memories from childhood ca[n] also contribute to collecting later in life. Now I have lots [of] *Pinocchios* and it still makes me happy to see their jol[ly] smiling faces. As much as I have always liked the imag[e] of Walt Disney's Pinocchio, the first time I saw the fil[m] was when I purchased the video several years ago. [Pi]nocchio is an artistic and innovative movie and is no[w] considered one of Disney's great classics, but I wou[ld] rather remember the *Pinocchio* whose adventures I cre[ated myself by playing with the doll.

There is no end of dolls to collect. That is why [it] always continues to be so much fun. I also like to colle[ct] paper dolls and to create original ones. One of my ear[ly] ones is shown in this book.

In 1990, I was honored with the Award of Excellenc[e] in Research and Writing by the International Doll Acad[emy. This was a wonderful honor and I am pleased th[at] other researchers appreciate my work. I began to do [it] because I wanted to know more about the things tha[t I] like so much. I am fortunate that a publishing compan[y,] Hobby House Press, Inc., was interested in printing m[y] findings and that other collectors see something of valu[e] in them.

John Axe
31 March 1991

Editor's Note: If you have enjoyed reading these article[s] by John Axe, you are invited to subscribe to **Doll Reade[r]** magazine for additional articles on doll collecting topi[cs] of interest.

CHILD STAR DOLLS
OF THE 1930S & 1940S

Anne Shirley (born 1918) from ca. 1923 when she was child star Dawn O'Day.

All-original *Anne Shirley* by EFFANBEE in the late 1930s wearing a pale pink sheer cotton dress. (It is possible she is from the early 1940s, which would make her a "Little Lady" rather than Anne Shirley.) She is 14in. (35.6cm) and has a brown human hair wig, blue sleep eyes and the large hands of the Anne Shirley doll. The head is not marked, the torso is embossed: EFFANBEE//ANNE SHIRLEY.

UNESCO (United Nations Educational, Scientific, and Cultural Organization) has proclaimed 1979 the International Year of the Child. The United States, like the other participating nations, will observe this project. International Year of the Child is stimulating attention and concern regarding the needs of children all over the world, especially in the developing countries.

For doll collectors, every year is the Year of the Child. Most doll collections feature dolls of children and babies that are loved more than many real children are. No true doll collector ever lives a day during which he or she does not think of their collection or do some work in connection with it. Without a doubt, doll collectors will take an active part in the awarness program to aid children, whether it be by support of the UNESCO project or in their own personal way.

The all-composition dolls included in this photographic essay are dolls of some of the most famous and popular children of all time. The dolls are portraits of child movie actresses from the 1930s and the 1940s who earned tremendous adult attention, interest and admiration because of their celebrity status. There are no contemporary children who have achieved the fame and popularity of the children who were the inspiration for these dolls. We will probably never again see so many famous children capture public adulation in a single generation as these did.

Who would not envy having a collection such as the one shown here? And these acclaimed children of a past era help to make us more aware of those unfortunate children all over the world in our own time.

Shirley Temple (born 1927) from the 1934 fi[lm]
Eyes. The doll Shirley is holding is probably a P[...]
by EFFANBEE. The doll in Jane Withers' arms [is]
a LENCI.

Above:
All-original 16in. (40.6cm) *Shirley Temple* by IDEAL.
This is the "knife-pleated" organdy dancing costume from
the film *Curly Top* in 1935. The dress is pink and is labeled; the underclothing has a paper label with "16" on
it. Head mark:

16
SHIRLEY TEMPLE
IDEAL
N. & T. Co.

Back mark:

SHIRLEY TEMPLE
16

Above right:
An imitator of the Shirley Temple doll is this 14in.
(35.6cm) HORSMAN *Bright Star.* She has a blond mohair
wig, blue tin sleep eyes and an open mouth with four
teeth. She is almost mint. The organdy dress is white with
red flowers and is trimmed in red. The doll is unmarked.
The tag in front that shows a doll that looks like the
Shirley Temple doll reads: HORSMAN'S//BRIGHT
STAR//"With eyes that shine//and hair so fine." The second tag, showing that is was probably a salesman's sample
carries the information: REGAL DOLL CORPORA-
TION//HORSMAN DOLLS, INC.//TRENTON, N.J.//
Style No. 526.

Right:
18in. (45.7cm) *Margaret O'Brien* in a labeled dress of heavy cotton from MADAME
ALEXANDER in 1946. She has a brown
mohair wig and blue sleep eyes. The hat is
original; the shoes and socks are replacements. The doll is marked both on the head
and back: ALEXANDER

6

Left:
17in. (43.2cm) *Jane Withers* doll by MADAME ALEXANDER with an open mouth that has teeth and a metal tongue. She, like most Jane Withers dolls, has an auburn mohair wig and green sleep eyes. The outfit is most likely a replacement. The head is marked: JANE WITHERS

ALEXANDER DOLL

The back is marked: 17
(*Lois Barrett Collection.*)

Right:
Jane Withers dolls were issued by MADAME ALEXANDER in various sizes in 1937. This 13in. (33cm) version is all-original in a tagged Jane Withers dress of pink organdy. She has an auburn mohair wig and green sleep eyes. The doll is not marked. (*Connie Chase Collection.*)

Margaret O'Brien (born 1937) in 1942. Margaret O'Brien was the last really popular child star; the doll was the last all-composition movie star doll.

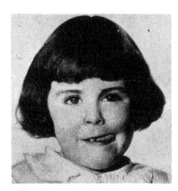

Juanita Quigley (born 1931) who performed in the movies under the name Baby Jane.

One of the most rare child movie star dolls and one of the most rare ALEXANDER dolls is *Baby Jane* from 1935. She is 17in. (43.2cm). She has an auburn mohair wig, brown glass-like sleep eyes, teeth and a metal tongue. The costume is not original. The head of the doll is marked: BABY-JANE//REG// Mme ALEXANDER
(*Betty Shriver Collection.*)

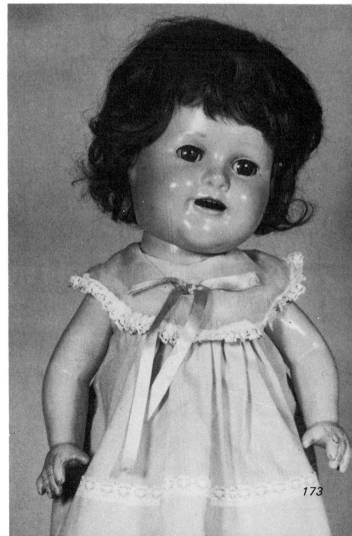

173

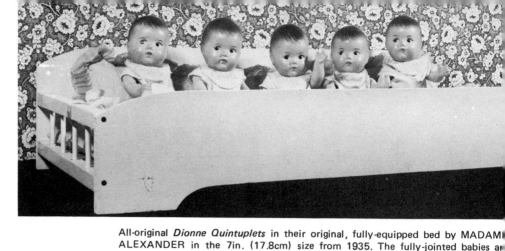

All-original *Dionne Quintuplets* in their original, fully-equipped bed by MADAM ALEXANDER in the 7in. (17.8cm) size from 1935. The fully-jointed babies are wearing diapers, undershirts and bibs. This is the "straight hair" 7in. (17.8cm) set with painted eyes which is marked ALEXANDER on the back and marked on the head: DIONNE//ALEXANDER

23in. (58.4cm) *Marie* with a cloth torso. The pink flannel coat and hat is an original Dionne outfit, but pink was the color for Yvonne in the ALEXANDER dolls. The white dress carries one of the more rare labels: DIONNE QUINTUPLETS//Marie// EXCLUSIVE LICENSEE//ALEXANDER DOLL CO. N.Y. The straight, painted hair, open mouth with teeth and the clothing dates the baby from 1935. The head is marked: "DIONNE"//ALEXANDER

Left:
From ca. 1937 is the all-composition Alexander toddler Dionne Quintuplet. This is an all-original *Yvonne* in a pink labeled dress of dotted swiss to which her name pin is attached. She has an open mouth with four teeth, brown sleep eyes and a human hair wig. Only the body is marked: ALEXANDER (*Lois Barrett Collection.*)

Right:
11-1/8in. (28cm) *Baby Sandy* by RALPH A. FREUNDLICH, INC., ca. 1940. She has yellow-painted hair and blue tin sleep eyes and an open mouth with two teeth and a felt tongue. The head is marked: BABY SANDY

Those Collectible Dolls In National Costume

Those Collectible Dolls in National Costume

In 1840, in England, for the first time the government issued postage stamps that would serve as prepayment for the delivery of letters. Many persons are reluctant to throw away anything that seems attractive to them and such small items as used postage stamps could easily be stored away. So, in a short time, saved stamps became an accumulation. Then when the accumulator deliberately set out to accumulate more stamps, the accumulation became a serious hobby.

Doll collecting can also follow this same pattern. The collecting of postage stamps and the collecting of dolls have other similarities. (The author knows several doll collectors who were once stamp collectors.) Outstanding among the parallels between collecting stamps and collecting dolls is that both groups of collectors soon educate themselves in other areas that do not pertain exclusively to the hobby.

The stamp collector usually begins by accumulating stamps of his own country. The doll collector begins by accumulating a few dolls that were relatively easy to acquire. Stamp collectors, once they become serious about collecting, realize that they can save thousands of stamps. Most doll collectors, when they seriously began collecting dolls, would not have believed that they would ever have 500 dolls in their collections at the time they began accumulating. Both groups, as their collections increase, learn things about their collections that they did not know would be a part of it. A stamp collector soon learns about the existence of countries all over the world that he had never heard of before. A doll collector cannot avoid learning about the outside world either. In fact, he or she will want to. There is scarcely a doll collector who will not want dolls manufactured in other countries or dolls that represent other nations in the collection. Both groups of collectors can consult encyclopedias and reference books to learn more about the countries from which parts of their collections came. Who is more curious about the origin of individual parts of a collection than the collector who is accumulating or collecting?

The dolls that can stimulate our curiosity the most are the foreign-made dolls or the dolls that represent persons of other nations. When one looks at a French doll, they do not just think of the doll. They also think of France.

Nowadays, people are exposed more and more to persons from other nations, even if the exposure only comes from viewing television. Most people, particularly in the Western World, tend to dress in the same manner and exhibit the same general styles. At the present time, it would be difficult to

Illustration 1. *6in (15cm) France. Most dolls that represent France are dressed in red and white striped skirts with black aprons and plain blouses and wear gold crosses at their necks. This is a variation of the folk dress of the northern French province of Bourbonnais. The doll is made from plastic, although the delicately toned and painted facial features and the blonde mohair wig give her the appearance of the classical Italian doll design made of stiffened cloth. This doll was a premium from Chef Boyardee spaghetti products in the early 1960s and is one of a large series of dolls in "foreign costumes" advertised as made in Italy with the offer. The doll also has a straw hat and a straw basket filled with felt flowers. Although unmarked, she appears to have been made in Italy by Eros, which manufactured similar dolls with an affixed label.*

determine an individual's social status, wealth or country of origin by observing how they dressed. Not long ago, especially in Europe, the ancestral home of many Americans, the costumes worn would differ drastically within regions of a country and would have little similarity between different nations. In many countries, costumes and styles were substantially different from region to region and even between villages within a given region.

Regional dress, or folk costume, evolved slowly over the centuries. Folk costume is in reality the "Sunday best" or the festival dress of the peasant class of a certain nation or region. Some of these typical folk costumes have become so closely identified with certain countries that people tend to think of them as the dress of that particular nation. Doll makers have dressed dolls that represent another nation in some popular folk costumes for so long that outsiders have become accustomed to believing that this is the national dress of that country.

Today, the main use of the peasant folk costume is for important festive occasions or for formal presentations of folk

Illustration 2. 11in (28cm) Brazil, *a Dream World doll. This doll is of fully-jointed composition with a mohair wig and blue painted. The dolls were retailed during the 1940s and are of a comparable mold to Madame Alexander dolls of that period. This doll is all-original and her clothing is stapled on. The original tag is attached to her left arm. The headdress is typical of Brazilian dress at carnival time preceding Lent. Dolls in this type of costume are erroneously referred to as Carmen Miranda, the Brazilian movie actress who attained popularity in the 1940s, but they were no doubt deliberately dressed as Carmen Miranda to cash in on her popularity.*

Illustration 3. 11in (28cm) Sweden. *The tag is missing on this Dream World doll dressed in a version of typical peasant dress from Sweden. The original box carries no company markings but is stamped: "No. 34 Swedish." She also wears a small black cap and under her satin skirt has the same undergarments of stiffened cheesecloth and wears shoes and socks as other Dream World dolls. Like most of the dolls of this series from an American manufacturer whose origins are so far untraceable, the doll has remained in "mint condition" although these dolls were produced to retail at a modest price.*

music and folk dances. Men from Scotland do not drive off to work in a factory wearing a kilt, nor do ladies in Spain prance about in public with trailing ruffled skirts, clicking castanets with their fingers. Yet dolls of the Scots usually wear kilts and most dolls representing Spain are dressed as flamenco dancers. The dolls that depict persons of other nations are seldom dressed authentically. However, they do demonstrate the flavor of the nation as found in its historical regional traditions. Little dolls representing the Netherlands wear wooden shoes although modern girls in Amsterdam never thought to try on a pair. However, the dolls in national dress, in their own way, help to preserve many traditions and folk ways of the past.

We learn of other countries and of other ideas by accident and by design once our accumulation becomes organized into a collection. To a stamp collector, foreign postage stamps are often the most intriguing aspect of the entire collection. The "international" doll, or the doll dressed in a regional or national costume, will find its way into almost every collection "from bisque to vinyl" because doll manufacturers have always realized that a series of their products will induce more sales, just as collectors know that a series of these dolls can enhance their own expanding collections.

Even the United States has what could be classified as national dress. The most "typical" costume is, no doubt, the attire of the Old West, the outfits of cowboys, which were designed for practicality and which include influences from many different cultures, like the colorfully embroidered shirts of the peasant costumes of Europe, and aspects of Spanish, Mexican and Indian dress. Doll makers dress dolls as cowboys and cowgirls so that they obviously represent Americans. Scores of different types of Indian dolls have also been made over the years to represent the true native American people.

Travelers to different parts of the United States have accumulated Indian dolls as souvenirs of their trips as travelers to outside nations have been enchanted with a doll that reminds them of the foreign place that they enjoyed. These reminders of pleasant experiences can be turned into a doll

Illustration 4. 10in (25cm) Guardia Civil, *from the Linda Pirula factory in Spain. This doll is part of a large series of dolls in typical Spanish costume and is unusual in that it is a current product [late 1970s] and is made of fully-jointed hard plastic. The Spanish Guardia Civil would compare to the American state patrol and the doll wears a faithful rendition of the olive green uniform. He has a glued-on brown wig and green flirty eyes.*

Illustration 5. 17¼in (44cm) Torero Revolera *from Spain. The most famous of the Spanish character dolls are those designed by José Marín Verdugo. This* Torero Revolera *(literally, a bullfighter turning in front of a bull with a large matador's cape) is rendered from vinyl with clothing fitted and sewed to the doll and demonstrates the unique Marín concept of designing dolls. The* Torero, *who is wearing a blue costume, has a correctly proportioned adult figure rather than being childlike as seen with the Pirula doll shown in* Illustration 4. *The Marín tag, sewed to the cape, reads, on the reverse side: "Torero Revolera//ref 262."*

Illustration 6. 9in (23cm) Joven Zamorano *from Spain, by Marín. This doll, with a tag reading "ref 529," is dressed in typical regional peasant attire from the province of Zamora in western Spain. The suit is brown corduroy and the figure carries a wooden shepherd's staff. No young man of Zamora (joven zamorano) has, needless to say, worn this sort of costume for many years.*

Illustration 7. 6½in (17cm) Alentejano. *This doll is a farmer from the Alentejo region of eastern Portugal, where the typical landscape is one of vast expanses of wheat fields. The doll wears a "fur" vest and pants, as the Alentejo is subject to the worst extremes of temperature in all Portugal. The doll carries a lunch container made of cork, which is the bark of the cork tree, one of Portugal's chief export products.*

Although both Spain and Portugal share the Iberian Peninsula, the most southern area of Europe, the two nations have few mutual interests as they have always been in competition with each other. Portugal, like Spain, has many beautiful regional traditions that are preserved in dolls dressed in folk costumes from long ago. This doll and the other hard plastic dolls shown in Illustrations 8 through 10 are from Portugal and while they are not marked, the province or the character they represent is stamped on the base. They have painted features, are fully-jointed with swivel waists and are all glued to a cork base.

Illustration 8. 6½in (17cm) Algarvio. *The Algarve is the southern tip of Portugal which faces Africa. Its folk customs, like those of southern Spain, are derived in part from the Arabs who occupied the area from 711 until 1297. The Algarvios have traditionally divided their means of earning a livelihood between the soil and the sea, although the area in recent times has developed a seaside resort industry. This doll, wearing typical peasant dress, is playing the concertina.*

collection. The non-traveler can also accumulate dolls dressed in folk costumes and, like the person who began saving postage stamps by 1841, will soon discover that he is also a collector. However, a doll dressed in the costume of another nation is far more "alive" than a tiny photograph showing that area of the world, even if it would deliver a letter! ☐

Illustration 9. 6¹/₂in (17cm) Lavadeira. *Portugal is probably the poorest country of western Europe although the standard of living has improved since the "Bloodless Revolution" of 1974. In some rural areas, lavadeiras (laundresses) still [in the 1970s] wash clothing in streams of pure unspoiled water. Modern young women scorn the custom, but a practical way of carrying large bundles is to balance them on the head. This is facilitated by forming a ring of twisted cloth and placing it on the head under the package to add balance.*

Illustration 10. 6¹/₂in (17cm) Galinheira. *The English equivalent of a* galinheira *would be a poulterer or a raiser/seller of chickens. The doll has a basket balanced on her head in which she is carrying a chicken to market. A tiny ceramic rooster is inside the basket. The rooster, shown in* Illustration 11, *is brightly painted and is a common motif in Portuguese craftsmanship and decoration.*

Illustration 11. *The doll would not want just any old chicken in her basket and so a Barcelos Rooster is in her basket which adds to her own legend! The Barcelos Rooster, a symbol of Portugal, is derived from a religious legend. In the town of Barcelos in the province of Minho, a serious crime was committed. The criminal could not be located and, in the meantime, a Spaniard from nearby Galicia appeared in town. The authorities decided that the foreigner must be the culprit so he was arrested and sentenced to death. The stranger insisted that he was innocent and that he was just a pilgrim on his way to the shrine of Saint James in Spain. The man begged to speak with the judge who had sentenced him before he was to be hanged. The Galician was taken before the judge who was seated in his dining room preparing to carve a roasted chicken. The condemned man told the judge, "When you hang me that rooster will crow to prove to you that I am innocent." Everyone laughed at the man but the judge lost his appetite for roasted chicken. The prisoner was led away to be hanged. Just as the rope was put around the neck of the man who had been sentenced, the rooster lifted its head off the plate in front of the judge and crowed loudly. The judge rushed to the gallows and discovered in astonishment that the man he had sentenced to death was hanging from the rope but he was still alive and still professing his innocence. The judge immediately ordered the pilgrim to be set free and let him continue on his way to the shrine of Saint James where he gave thanks for the miracle that had saved him from death in Portugal.*

Shirley Temple Dolls

Illustration 2. 22in (55.9cm). *Shirley Temple* as *Heidi*, 1937, from the film dream sequence in which she sang and danced as a Dutch girl. This all-original doll is one of the rarest of the Composition versions. *Patricia Slabe Collection.*

FIRST SHIRLEY TEMPLE DOLL

$3.79
15-Inch

"I Sleep"

Give Her a Shirley Temple Doll and Make Her Happy on Christmas

It's Shirley Temple, adorable dimples, curly hair and all. Even her dress is just like the one Shirley wears in the movies—coin-dot organdy, and she wears dainty undies, shoes and socks and a ribbon in her hair. She has **hazel eyes (glass-like, unbreakable) with real lustrous lashes;** a smiling mouth that shows her pearly teeth and her tongue-tip, and curly hair just the shade of Shirley's. She's all of hard-to-break composition with tilting head, moveable arms and legs. **Shirley can stand alone and go to sleep.** One of Shirley's favorite Hollywood photographs with each doll and a Shirley Temple button. Again Sears are first with the newest—Shirley Temple dolls are sold by mail only by Sears.

Illustration 1. One of the first advertisements for the *Shirley Temple* dolls, *Sears 1934 Christmas Catalog.*

One of the most important dolls in the history of doll collecting is the *Shirley Temple* doll from Ideal, first issued 50 years ago in time for Christmas of 1934. The lasting popularity and desirability of this doll is the best indication of the tremendous success and adulation of the child film star Shirley Temple.

In 1936, 1937 and 1938 little Shirley Temple was the Number One Box Office Star in the movies. No child has ever rivaled her fame. Within her lifetime she was the single most famous child in the history of the world and the seventh highest paid person in the United States. Her films were escapist fare that audience during the Depression loved, ar these 1930s movies are still shown o television every week. Shirley Temp retired from the movies in 1950 b everyone still knows who she is. April of 1984 she was the first pr senter at the annual Academy Awar ceremony and at age 56 she still h her dimples, her sparkle, her beau and her perky personality. A thousar years from now people will still kno who Shirley Temple was.

For many years, *Shirley Temp* dolls have been eagerly sought collectors, the most desirable dolls all being the composition dolls fro

Illustration 3. 20in (50.8cm) *Shirley Temple* baby, 1935. Composition head on a shoulder plate; composition arms and legs; stuffed cloth body. Flirty sleep eyes with lashes; two upper teeth and three lower teeth. Head marked: "SHIRLEY TEMPLE." *Barbara DeVault Collection.*

BELOW: Illustration 4. 35in (88.9cm) vinyl version from the late 1950s. *Wanda Lodwick Collection.*

he 1930s, with a couple of notable xceptions. Shirley Temple is also one f the few motifs upon which entire— nd very large—collections are built. o *Shirley Temple* doll was ever an ccurate "portrait" of the little star, ut the composition dolls captured her ssence and her charm perfectly. The nly other dolls that many collectors el reflect the real Shirley Temple are e 35in (88.9cm) vinyl edition from 957-1960 and the 16¾in (42.6cm) nyl doll from 1973.

Another indication of how tre- endously popular the *Shirley emple* dolls were in their own time is ll of the look-alike and knock-off dolls at were made in composition during e 1930s, and even copies of the vinyl olls of the late 1950s. In the 1930s e composition dolls were not reason- bly priced items for little girls. In one f the first advertisements for the olls, *Sears 1934 Christmas Catalog* sted the 15in (38.1cm) size for $3.79. family of four could eat for a week for at much money then!

The success of the composition hirley Temple dolls immediately rompted other American doll com- anies to market their own versions of child film star doll. A good example of is is Effanbee's *Anne Shirley* of 934 and Madame Alexander's *Baby*

Illustration 5. 17in (43.2cm) from the late 1950s. She is all-vinyl and carries her original "autographed" purse. *Wanda Lodwick Collection.*

Jane (Quigley) of 1935. As wonderful, and popular, as these other dolls may have been, the little girls really wanted a *Shirley Temple* doll first. Many of them had to wait about 30 years to get their first *Shirley Temple* doll. And it was usually not their last! It was the beginning of a collection.

Another trend that the Shirley Temple dolls developed more than any other doll was the tradition of the Celebrity Doll. Doll companies have been trying for years to emulate the success of the *Shirley Temple* doll by producing dolls of other popular and successful celebrities, especially dolls of entertainment personalities. No other doll has come close to rivaling the *Shirley Temple* doll, although dolls of other performers have been very successful and collectible.

We are in the midst of another surge of popularity of Celebrity Dolls and many different celebrities are currently rendered as dolls. This sort of doll will always be one of the most desirable and collectible because everyone knows whom the doll represents. It is not just another doll with a doll's name. At the present time Ideal is issuing another round of Shirley Temple dolls.

Shirley Temple herself has not performed for almost 25 years, but as a doll she is timeless because she was the very personification of childhood at its best and most nostalgic. And nostalgia is the basis of all doll collecting. □

SHIRLEY TEMPLE DOLLS FROM IDEAL

Year	Material	Type	Sizes
1934 to about 1939	All-composition	child	12 sizes from 9 inches (22.9cm) to 27 inches (68.6cm)
1935	Composition and cloth	baby	6 sizes from 14 inches (35.6cm) to 27 inches (68.6cm)
circa 1950	Hard plastic	child	15 inches (38.1cm)
1957 to 1960	All-vinyl	child	5 sizes from 12 inches (30.5cm) to 35 inches (88.9cm)
1972	All-vinyl	child	14 inches (35.6cm)
1973	Vinyl and plastic	child	16¾ inches (42.6cm)
1982-1983	All-vinyl	child	8 inches (20.3cm) and 12 inches (30.5cm)
1983-1984	Porcelain	child	16 inches (40.6cm)
1984	All-vinyl	child	16 inches (40.6cm)

hirley Temple Dolls

All-composition *Shirley Temple* dolls in various sizes.

Illustration 1. All-cloth *Kewpies*. They are 10¾in (27.4cm) and 17½in (44.5cm). Both dolls have painted mask faces.

KEWPIE

Kewpie is one of the most beloved doll motifs of the twentieth century. The *Kewpies* were designed in 1909 by Rose O'Neill as drawings for *The Woman's Home Companion*. Rose O'Neill contracted the young sculptor Joseph Kallus to translate her designs into doll form. The first dolls were made in bisque in 1913 in Germany. Since that time *Kewpie* has been made by many different German and American doll firms in all sorts of doll mediums — bisque, celluloid, cloth, composition, hard plastic, vinyl and others. In 1983, after about a ten year absence, *Kewpie* came back again in three different vinyl renditions manufactured by Jesco, a doll company in California.

Rose O'Neill's *Kewpie* was inspired by Cupid from Greek mythology. Cupid (or Eros) was a small but powerful god of love and he was the son of Venus, the goddess of love, and her constant companion. With his bows and arrows, Cupid shot the darts of desire into the bosoms of gods and men. Rose O'Neill told children in 1909 that *Kewpie* was a "pet name" for Cupid. She added, "But there is a difference. Cupid gets himself in trouble. The Kewpies get themselves out, always searching out ways to make the world better and funnier."

The *Kewpies* shown here in the **DOLL READER**™ have made the world "better and funnier." Many of them are from the collection of Wanda Lodwick, as are many of the old Valentines. These Valentines were all printed in Germany and they were sent to people in the early 1920s. □

Illustration 2. Composition *Kewpies* from the 1940s. At the left: 11in (27.9cm) with jointed arms and painted blue wings on the back. The heart label is on the chest. At the right: 13in (33cm) and fully jointed in an original sunsuit. These fully-jointed versions were licensed by Cameo and made and distributed by Effanbee.

Illustration 3. Left to Right: Three all-vinyl *Kewpies* from the late 1960s-early 1970s, probably by Amsco (Milton Bradley), under license from Joseph Kallus' Cameo Doll Company. They are 6in (15.2cm), 10in (25.4cm) and 14in (35.6cm).

NEXT PAGE: Illustration 4. All-hard plastic *Kewpie* from the 1950s. 8½in (21.6cm) with jointed arms and molded wings on the back.

All-bisque *Kewpies* with jointed arms, from the early 20th century, 5in (13cm), 6½in (16cm) and 10in (25cm) tall. They are all incised on the bottom of their feet: "O'NEILL." *Wanda Lodwick, Collection.*

Exclusive Doll Reader™ Interview With Madame Alexander

In late November 1983 we had the special privilege of interviewing Madame Alexander in her home in Florida. This is our report of that event.

*

Madame Alexander celebrated her 89th birthday on March 9, 1984. But that is just a chronological fact. Physically and mentally she has probably changed very little in the past 89 years. She is still thin and beautiful. Her hands are as soft and smooth as those of a child, and it is hard to believe that she has been working with them most of her life.

Her apartment is decorated in a French style, a reflection of her own "Old World" elegance. In the living room some of her most famous dolls are on display. This includes *Goya*, *Queen Elizabeth*, *Scarlett* and *Melanie* in the "Portrait"

series. In the den there are cases with a nice assortment of the "Portrettes" that use the *Cisette* doll. The outer part of the guest bathroom has a large display of the 8 inch (20.3cm) "International Dolls" as a wall decoration. Other aspects of the decor include a doll motif, like the oil paintings done by her daughter, Mildred. To many collectors Madame Alexander is a "star," and like the great film stars she has special closets that catalog her extensive collection of gowns and shoes that she uses for her many public appearances.

Madame Alexander was seated on a white sofa with her little poodle companion, Duchess, at her side as she answered our questions and told us about her long career, all of which came from her astonishing memory.

* * * * * * *

DR: *Madame Alexander, where were you born?*

MADAME ALEXANDER: I was born in Brooklyn, New York, on March 9 1895, and taken to Grand Street, New York, when three years old.

DR: *Did you come from a large family?*

MADAME ALEXANDER: I had three younger sisters.

The elegant Madame Alexander with one of her favorite dolls, Scarlett. Some of the Madame's beautiful porcelain collection is shown in the background.

DR: *As a child what were your favorite playthings? Did you like dolls?*

MADAME ALEXANDER: I never had any dolls. My three younger sisters took the place of dolls. I always liked fine porcelain vases and antiques and I developed a love and respect for these things from the time I was very young. My father repaired antiques and later specialized in repairing dolls, so I grew up around these things, which I still love. I didn't have many things of my own, but I was always satisfied with what I had.

DR: *Did you have any special hobbies?*

MADAME ALEXANDER: I was always a great reader from the time I was a young girl. I loved the books of Louisa May Alcott and Charles Dickens, and later when I began to make dolls I used the characters from this literature for my doll characters.

DR: *Did you train for any specialities as you were growing up?*

MADAME ALEXANDER: My family always placed great emphasis on education and in preparing the young for a profession. One of my uncles was an artist and another uncle was a teacher. I was the valedictorian of my class at Julia Richman High School. Then I went to business school. I wanted to get into the business world and earn a living, so I refused a teaching position that was offered to me at the business school.

DR: *What was your first position?*

MADAME ALEXANDER: When I was about 17 years old I was already engaged to my future husband, Phillip Berhman. I was offered a job at the Irving Hat Stores as a bookkeeper and I was making more money than he was at the time. We were married in 1913, at which time my husband was the head of personnel at a hat factory. He also worked at the Truly Warner Hat Shop on Broadway on Saturdays and was selling hats on the East Side on Sundays to make enough money. I always feared that the hat business might have problems and I remembered the time in 1911 when my parents lost their savings when the bank in which they had their money failed.

DR: *Is that what inspired you to go into business for yourself?*

MADAME ALEXANDER: Yes. I was worried about our financial future. And I was also involved in charity projects at the time that needed money. I was one of the ten original founders of *Keren Harpod* (later known as the Women's League for Israel). *Keren Harpod* helped young women by giving them a place to stay and to recover from the physical problems brought on by over-work and by trying to find jobs for them that were based

Madame Alexander reminisces about her life, career, and philosophies with her companion Duchess. Her semi-retirement has such benefits as the beautiful view of the sea from her condominium.

on their aptitudes. The government did not aid charities at this time and we needed more money to finance our projects, and my husband's salary was needed to support our family.

DR: *So you began the Alexander Doll Company. Did you ever think that your doll company would become the largest and most important of the American doll companies?*

MADAME ALEXANDER: Not at all. I didn't start out to have my dolls be

of any importance. I had certain goals, but I was relaxed about it and maybe this helped me to become successful. I began my company with a loan of $1,600.00 in 1923. After paying a month's rent in advance and buying some furniture and a sewing machine I was left with $826.00 to start my business. I didn't have enough money for tools and dies so the first doll I made was in muslin *Alice in Wonderland*. I sold the first 12 dolls for a wholesale price of $14.40. Stores objected that they could only sell

the dolls for $1.95 and that this was not a big enough mark-up for them to make a profit. So, I had to lower the price to $13.50 per dozen. The first real break that I had was when the lady who was the buyer for Wanamaker's bought some of my dolls. (Note: These *Alice in Wonderland* dolls that sold for $1.95 in 1923 are listed in the *5th Blue Book of Dolls & Values*™ at $300.00 to $350.00.)

DR: *Where did the Alexander Doll Company begin?*

MADAME ALEXANDER: We were first located on Grand Street in New York. We have been at our current factory facility for 30 years now.

DR: *What happened to make your dolls more popular and more in demand?*

MADAME ALEXANDER: Customers have always been our best salesmen. After people first saw my dolls they would first go into small stores -

The elegant *Madame Alexander* 21in (53.3cm) doll is to be released in 1984. *Madame* is attired in a floor-length pink evening gown, a cape with rhinestone accents and a rose corsage. The gorgeous wig is held in place by a pink velvet bow. Note the unusual drop pierced earrings. A remarkable doll made by a remarkable person.

department stores and ask, "Why don't you have Madame Alexander dolls?" Children themselves have been my press agents. Once when I was in the fitting room of Henri La Pensee trying on a gown I overheard two little girls talking as they were waiting for their mothers. One little girl asked the other, "Can I see your doll?" I was thrilled when the second little girl answered, "*This* is not just a doll. It is a Madame Alexander doll, you know."

DR: *Madame Alexander, of all the many dolls that you have made over the years, which is your favorite?*

MADAME ALEXANDER: Does a mother have a favorite among her children? If she does, will she tell? I remember how *Scarlett* was created. I began to read *Gone With the Wind* on a Friday evening and continued with the book until I had finished it by the end of the weekend. On Monday morning I went to work and by Wednesday I had created a doll from the description of *Scarlett* in the novel. She had a heart-shaped face, a small nose, green eyes, black hair and was one of my prettiest doll characters. And this was two years before Vivien Leigh was chosen to play the part in the film.

DR: *What other dolls did you create that enhanced your reputation and caused your company to become the leading American doll company?*

MADAME ALEXANDER: Dolls that were successful for me were the characters from the novels of Charles Dickens, like *Tiny Tim, David Copperfield, Little Nell* and *Little Dorrit*. These were cloth dolls with hand-painted faces. Another favorite and successful theme for my dolls was the four girls from *Little Women*. The dolls that brought me to the forefront of the doll industry were the *Dionne Quintuplets*. The Dionnes themselves were a phenomenon! The Quintuplet dolls were exceptional sellers for over four years. My other popular dolls were *Sonja Henie*, whose sales lasted for three years, and *Princess Elizabeth*, inspired from a portrait of Elizabeth when she was ten years old

DR: *What is your philosophy of what a Madame Alexander doll should be?*

MADAME ALEXANDER: I never do mechanical dolls. I don't make dolls that dance, walk or talk. I think that the child is the one who should be inspired to do things with the doll. Dolls can bring out the creative instincts in children. For example, if a little girl quietly relates stories to the doll it does this. The child can benefit more from this manner of playing and as an adult has learned to be entertained and amused without having other people do this for her.

DR: *Were your dolls created for little girls then?*

MADAME ALEXANDER: I believe that the maternal instinct is born in girls as the paternal instinct is born in boys.

My dolls speak to this beautiful, natural instinct. I don't believe that a doll should be pulled away from a little boy because he may become effeminate if he plays with dolls. He is also satisfying his feelings and natural instincts by playing with a doll.

DR: *But most of your dolls are ones that would appeal to girls, aren't they?*

MADAME ALEXANDER: Probably so. And realizing this I have never created anything nasty or ugly in my dolls. I wanted to inspire children with the doll creations I chose to make, and I wanted my dolls to be played with, not to be put away safely.

DR: *What do you think of the way that collectors have reacted to your dolls and the popularity that they have with collectors?*

MADAME ALEXANDER: Collectors have seen something special in my dolls that they appreciate, as do the children.

DR: *Madame, what was it like to be a woman in the very male dominated doll manufacturing world?*

MADAME ALEXANDER: In 1923 when I began to make dolls commercially it was a far different business environment than it is now. But I always attempted to be a lady and at the same time be a business person. This put me at a disadvantage with my competitors in the early years, but I believe that it has paid off in the end.

DR: *I think that everyone would agree with you.*

MADAME ALEXANDER: I have always believed in the philosophy that in order to be great you have to know how to be small. When one bakes a cake and uses the finest ingredients, one can expect to get good results!

DR: *Madame Alexander, it is apparent that you have the quiet reassurance of the value of your dolls to both children and to collectors. You have also been an excellent business person and at the same time a humanitarian and a philanthropist.*

MADAME ALEXANDER: Thank you. But I did not do all of it myself. I have always had the good fortune to employ the best craftsmen and many of them have been with our company for years. I have always had great respect for the employees of our company. We are the only company in the doll industry that keeps our people working on a year-round basis and we employ over 600 people. I have always tried to earn the respect of the people who worked for me, and take a personal interest in their problems. We have all been able to do our work to the best of our ability and I have always been blessed with a great deal of strength. I think that I have been successful because I did not work at my goals just to make money. I always believed in compulsory education and I think that there should also be compulsory employment for people.

DR: *Madame Alexander, even though you are now semi-retired do you still take a part in the business decisions of your company?*

MADAME ALEXANDER: I do, but I have turned most of the business operations of the company over to my son-in-law, Richard Birnbaum, and my grandson, William Alexander Birnbaum. They are managing the company excellently.

DR: *Would you tell us about your newest dolls for 1984?*

MADAME ALEXANDER: I have always insisted that every year there be a new doll in our line. This year there will be a *Madame Alexander* doll. I have been asked to do a doll of myself for many years but in my faith (Jewish) it is not considered good luck to name someone after a living person, and I have applied this to my dolls also. My husband did not want me to do a doll of myself, but my daughter Mildred talked me into it. She said, "Mother, do a doll of yourself and donate the profits from it to charity." So I have overlooked the superstitions because the sale of a doll of myself will allow me to do more charity work.

DR: *What is the* Madame Alexander *doll like?*

MADAME ALEXANDER: I traveled from my home in Florida to New York for several sittings with a sculptor who is in Brooklyn. He is the sculptor of the John F. Kennedy figure that is in Washington, D.C. at the Kennedy Center. My daughter, Mildred, designed the gown that the *Madame Alexander* doll wears. The design of the doll features pink, my favorite color. I presented the doll for the first time at Disney World on December 2, 1983, during a special appearance and, at Mildred's insistence, I wore a replica of the doll's gown. When it was announced in the newspapers that tickets would go on sale for my appearance at Disney World their phone circuits became overloaded! The Disney World people told me that I even outdrew Elvis Presley!

DR: *Has your daughter Mildred played an important part in your company?*

MADAME ALEXANDER: Mildred has always been a special part of my life. Because I was a working mother she had to assume many responsibilities at an early age. By the time she was twelve years old she could manage most of our household affairs. Mildred has always been completely unselfish and a great help to me. She, I am proud to say, has been recognized in *Who's Who in American Women*.

DR: *Madame Alexander, do you realize how important you are to doll collectors and to those who have always admired your work?*

MADAME ALEXANDER: I am a very lucky lady! □

Portraits of *Ginny* -- the 1950s

ABOVE: Illustration 1. Two *Ginnys* with molded lashes are in front of "Ginny's Wardrobe Trunk," which dates from 1955. The "Wardrobe Trunk" is metal-covered fiberboard. It came fitted with *Ginny* and various extra outfits, hats, hangers, slippers and play items and sold from $10.00 to $15.00. The wooden rocking chair in which a painted lash *Ginny* is seated, dates from 1957 when it sold for $2.00.

OPPOSITE PAGE: Illustration 2. *Ginnys* playing on "Ginny's Gym." Except for the two on the seesaw, who have molded lashes; the others have painted lashes. The boy at the left has a round tag that gives his name as *Jim*. The "Gym" was introduced in 1955 and originally sold for $8.00. It is clearly marked and is made of wood and pressed fiberboard.

Ginny® is a registered trademark of Vogue Dolls, Inc.

The hard plastic Vogue *Ginny* dolls from the 1950s have become more desirable than ever as collectibles. It is not unusual to see the earlier dolls in mint-in-the-box condition priced in excess of $200.00 now. *Ginny* was advertised as "the fashion leader in doll society" and the original costumes and the accessory costumes for *Ginny* from the 1950s seem to have been made in greater numbers than those from any other doll of the period. Jennie H. Graves began her Vogue Doll Shoppe, which dressed dolls, in 1922. By the 1950s this became Vogue Dolls, Inc., one of the most important doll manufacturers of the period. By the 1960s the *Ginny* dolls were made with vinyl components, and although they were still cute play dolls they had lost much of their original charm. In the summer of 1982 it was announced that Vogue Dolls (a division of Lesney AMT Corporation) was "going out of business" and collectors might not see new *Ginny* dolls for some time.

The following dating system for hard plastic *Ginny* dolls is adapted from *That Doll, Ginny,* copyright 1978 by Jeanne Du Chateau Niswonger:

Illustration 3. Advertisem[ent] from *Playthings,* April 19[5]. *Ginny's* wire-haired terrier w[as] made in Germany by Steiff a[nd] retailed for $2.00. The *gir[l]* pictured has painted lashes[;] dating *Ginny* dolls there [is] always an overlap in time [of] the various models.

Date	Description	Marks
1948 to 1950	Painted eyes; mohair wigs	Head: VOGUE Back: VOGUE DOLL
1950 to 1953	Sleep eyes with painted lashes; synthetic (usually Dynel) wigs	Head: VOGUE Back: VOGUE DOLL
1952 only	Same as the above with "poodle cut" hair of lamb's wool	Head: VOGUE Back: VOGUE DOLL
1954	Walking mechanism added	Head: VOGUE Back: GINNY VOGUE DOLLS INC. PAT. PEND. MADE IN U.S.A.
1955	Plastic eyelashes added	Head: VOGUE Back: GINNY VOGUE DOLLS INC. PAT. NO. 2687594 MADE IN U.S.A.
1957-1963	Bending knees added to the above	

Illustration 4. Blue painted eye *Cowgir[l]* and *Cowboy* with blonde mohair wigs. The shirts and hats are red; the vests are green felt; her skirt is white leatherette; his chaps are lamb's wool. Her shoes are replaced. They should be red leatherette with center snaps.

The *Ginny* dolls in hard plastic are all approximately 8in (20.3cm) tall.

Illustration 5. *Ginny* with a brown mohair wig and blue painted eyes.

Illustration 7. *Ginny* wearing a costume called "Holly Belle," 1951. The wig is a reddish-blonde; the eyes are brown. The hat and the yoke of the dress are red velvet; the white taffeta skirt is trimmed with felt holly. There is a "Christmas bell" attached to the panties.

Illustration 6. *Jim, Ginny* as *Bo Peep* and *Ginny*, all with brown sleep eyes and painted lashes. All three dolls have Dynel wigs. *Bo Peep* has dark brown hair; the others have blonde hair. The vinyl shoes are marked "GINNY" and were not used until 1955. The "personalized head band" worn by the *Ginny* on the right dates from 1958.

8in (20cm) *Ginny* dolls by Vogue, 1950 to 1953, dressed as a cowgirl and an Indian. The cowgirl has gray-blue sleep eyes with painted eyelashes while the Indian girl has brown sleep eyes with painted eyelashes. Their heads are marked "VOGUE" and their backs are marked "VOGUE DOLL."

Illustration 10. *Ginny* walker with plastic eyelashes and blue sleep eyes. The hair is dark brown. The felt jumper and matching hat are blue.

:ration 8. Blonde and red-haired *Ginnys* with lamb's wool wigs in the "poodle cut." Both have blue eyes.

Illustration 9. *Ginny* walkers with plastic eyelashes. All of the dolls pictured have blue eyes. The *Ginny* at the left with bending knees is wearing a Greek costume that was packaged in a Vogue box. "Ginny's Costumes from Far-Away Lands" were sold in boxed sets representing various foreign countries in 1958; in 1968 this costume was shown on one of the "Ginny Dolls from Far-Away Lands." The other three *Ginnys* are wearing outfits from the mid 1950s.

Collectible Black Dolls

10³/₄in (27cm) jet black unmarked girl with a straw-stuffed body, shoulder plate head and lower arms and legs of painted papier-mâché; black mohair wig which has been replaced; black glass eyes with no pupils, open/closed mouth with painted teeth; dress appears to be original, as the upper arms are made from the identical material. Lois Barrett Collection.

Black dolls, contrary to the belief of some black entertainers who appear on television talk shows, have been manufactured since the inception of mass-produced dolls in the last century. The bisque-headed dolls from Germany and France around the turn of the century often depicted blacks as Africans and were notable for their authentic Negroid modeling and quality construction. By contrast, American-made black dolls before World War I often carried such names as *Darky*, *Mammy* and *Dusky Dude* and the advertising capitalized on the comical aspects of these dolls and toys. Generally, during the 1920s, 1930s and 1940s, black dolls were cheaply and crudely made and were frequently (especially in composition) a dark painted version of the same white doll. During the 1950s, black dolls remained, for the most part, "colored" versions of standard dolls. Not until the 1960s were black dolls in the United States being mass-produced to truly represent black people. (The period also coincided with new legislation that extended civil rights to black Americans.)

The Black Experience in America has been far from pleasant. Aside from the time of slavery itself, the years following the Civil War, which delivered Blacks from human bondage, were probably the worst. Burnings, lynchings and maimings were not uncommon and were not confined to the South. Following 1877, when the South was permitted by the conquering North to resume its own ways, segregation once again became the order of society to prevent the black population from becoming a political force.

For almost another century, in the South and in the North, blacks were ridiculed and denigrated in literature, on the stage and in the movies. Entire generations of Americans viewed them as simple-minded, childlike and ignorant stereotypes who were frequently referred to as "coons," "jigs" or worse. In D. W. Griffith's *The Birth of a Nation*, which is now regarded as a great film classic, they were portrayed as wild savages. In a great many subtle and often innocent ways, white children were taught these attitudes by the books they read and the toys they played with.

The most prolific American writer ever was Edward Stratemeyer. He turned out an astounding 950 books under dozens of different pseudonyms and these books were always widely read by American children. (Stratemeyer's pseudonym for the Bobbsey Twins series is Laura Lee Hope. The books are copyrighted and printed by Grosset & Dunlap, New York.) Stratemeyer edited 18 of Horatio Alger's books in the last part of the 19th century (after Alger's death) and personally scripted or outlined most of the popular children's series books of the first 30 years of this century. He was the author of about 40 series of juvenile fiction including *The Rover Boys, Tom Swift, The Six Little Bunkers, The Bobbsey Twins, Nancy Drew, The Hardy Boys* and *Bomba, the Jungle Boy*.

Edward Stratemeyer showed children a positive, affirmative and enthusiastic view of American life and American cultural values. In his idealized conception of growing up, there was always hope in the future and the belief that "living right paid off." Stratemeyer died in 1930 and his daughter, Harriet Stratemeyer Adams, carried on his

work, continuing to assign outlined books to ghost writers who filled in the details. The Nancy Drew series alone has sold about 50 million copies to date [1978].

The books that are still being distributed have been updated to eliminate many anachronisms. Magic lantern showings have been converted to television viewings. Stereotyped characters, such as different ethnic groups, are no longer set off by the use of dialect. The 1904 edition of the first volume of the Bobbsey Twins series, *The Bobbsey Twins or Merry Days Indoors and Out*, showed the black person in the same light as did most of the dolls and toys of the time. In this original edition of the series, the black servants of the family were explained as:

"Sam was the man of all work. He and Dinah, the cook, were married and lived in some pleasant rooms over the stable." (Page 21)

In the 1961 edition of the book, now called *The Bobbsey Twins of Lakeport*, Dinah is still described as a "jolly-looking colored woman" but her status has been elevated:

"She was Dinah Johnson who helped Mrs. Bobbsey with the housework. Her husband Sam drove a truck at Mr. Bobbsey's lumberyard. Dinah and Sam lived in an apartment on the third floor of the Bobbsey house and were very popular with the whole family." (Page 4)

Dinah's speech has changed a great deal over the years also. When Freddie's snow house collapsed on him in the 1904 book this was Dinah's reaction:

" 'Gracious sakes alive, chile!' burst out Dinah, and without waiting to put anything on her head she rushed forth into the garden. 'Gib me dat shovel quick! He'll be stuffocated fo' yo' know it!' " (Page 52)

In the 1950 updated edition of the book, Dinah spoke differently:

" 'Gracious sakes alive, child!' burst out Dinah, and without waiting to put on a coat she rushed out into the garden. 'Give me that shovel quick! He'll be suffocated before you know it!' " (Page 53)

The 1961 edition of the book eliminated the snow house scene and Dinah talked this way:

" 'How would you all like a picnic lunch?' " (Page 4)

" 'You boys get upstairs and take hot showers and get into pajamas and robes.' " (Page 116)

The most telling sequence that shows how the black person was viewed over the years in the Bobbsey Twins books is in the description of Flossie's dolls, from the 1904 book:

"Flossie's dolls were five in number. Dorothy was her pride, and had light hair and blue eyes, and three dresses, one of real lace. The next was Gertrude, a short doll with black eyes and hair and a traveling dress that was very cute. Then came Lucy, who had lost one arm, and Polly who had lost both an arm and a leg. The fifth doll was Jujube, a colored boy, dressed in a fiery suit of red, with a blue cap and real rubber boots. This doll had come from Sam and Dinah and had been much admired at first, but was now taken out only when all the others went too.

" 'He doesn't really belong to the family, you know,' Flossie would explain to her friends. 'But I have to keep him, for mamma says there is no colored orphan asylum for dolls. Besides, I don't think Sam and Dinah would like to see their doll child in any asylum.' The dolls were all kept in a row in a big bureau drawer at the top of the house, but Flossie always took pains to separate Jujube from the rest by placing the cover of a pasteboard box between them." (Pages 56 to 57)

There was no more Jujube by 1950 as is shown in this excerpt:

"The fifth doll was a clown, dressed in bright yellow with large red polka dots and with enormous shoes. His name was Calico, and he had a huge mouth which extended from ear to ear.

" 'Calico is always laughing,' Flossie would explain to her friends.

" 'He gets into mischief sometimes and I had to spank him once. It was the time he fell into Dinah's cookie batter. But even then he still smiled, and I was sorry that I had punished him.' " (Page 57)

The black person has gained a more equal position in American society since the turn of the century and so have black dolls. For Christmas of 1977, many black dolls were advertised, such as *Beautiful Tara* in the J. C. Penney Catalog and glamourous *Malibu Christie*® from Mattel. There are black celebrity dolls of contemporary favorites like comedian Redd Foxx and singer-actress Diana Ross. Black dolls are now created, manufactured and advertised under the same standards as white dolls. Therefore, black dolls have truly become "little people."

Opposite: 13 Inch boy with a head and half-arms of early composition. All the facial features are painted and the doll is not marked although it may be a HORSMAN. The body is stuffed cloth with the legs attached by metal disks and also jointed at the knees. The clothing and the felt shoes appear to be original. *The Rodolfos Collection.*

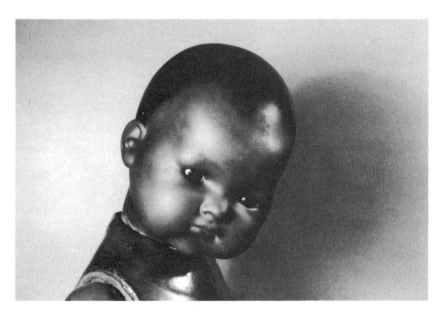

Solid dome, bisque-head *Dream Baby* by ARMAND MARSEILLE in the 24 inch size. She has brown sleep eyes and a closed mouth. The 15 inch circumference head is marked:

> A. M.
> Germany (in script lettering)
> 341./8.K.

The five-piece papier mâché body is marked on the back:

Barbara DeVault Collection.

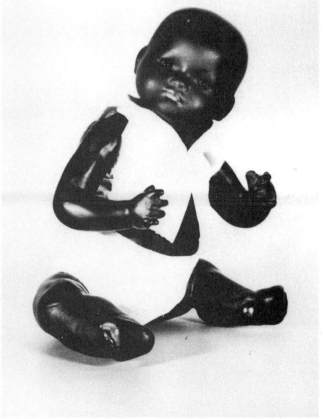

11 Inch *Dream Baby* with an 8-1/4 inch circumference head marked:

> A. M.
> GERMANY
> 341/O.K.

The body is composition and is not original to the doll. *Lois Barrett Collection.*

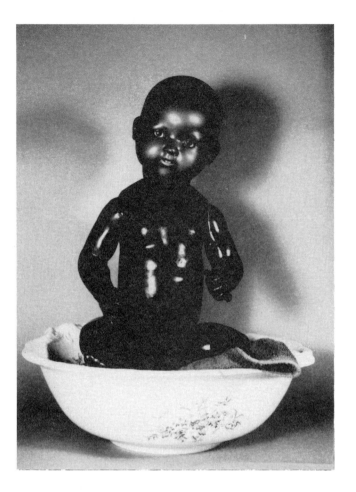

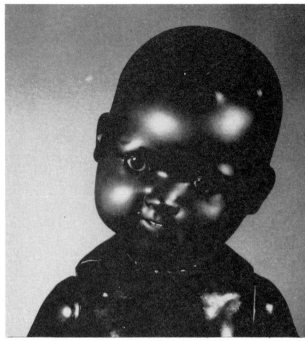

Above Left and Right: The AM 351 *Rockaby Baby*, also known as the *Open-Mouth Dream Baby.* The overall length is 22-1/4 inches and the head measures 15-1/2 inches in circumference. The baby has a five-piece composition body, brown glass sleep eyes, two lower teeth and painted black hair. The head is marked:

A. M.

GERMANY

351./8.k.

Wanda Lodwick Collection.

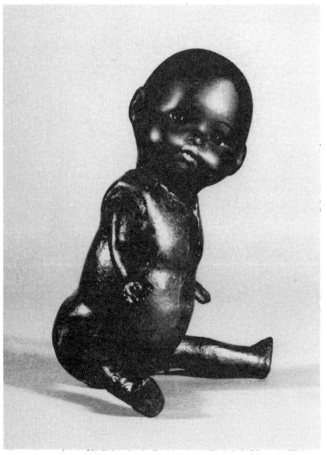

Left: 8 Inch solid-bisque head baby on a jointed papier mâché body that has thin arms and legs and an unusually chubby torso. She has black sleep eyes and an open mouth with two lower teeth. The head is marked:

roreig

344. 17/o

Fay and Jimmy Rodolfos Collection.

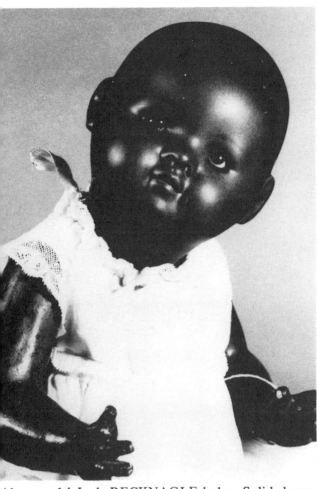

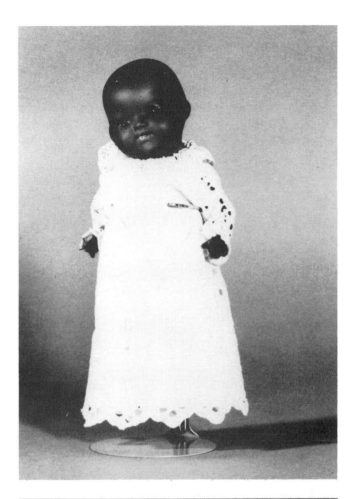

Above: 14 Inch RECKNAGLE baby. Solid dome head on a five-piece baby body of papier mâché, with very "bent" arms. The black sleep eyes have no pupils. The head is marked:
GERMANY
3½
Rl38A

Above Right: AM 351 *Rockabye Baby*. This version is 8 inches and is constructed like the Rockabye pictured on page 6. Her head is marked:
A.M.
GERMANY
351 5/O.K.

Right: 9 Inch *Dream Baby* with a solid-bisque head, composition half-arms and a cloth body with a squeaker inside. The head is a light brown color, 6-1/2 inches in circumference and is marked:
A.M.
GERMANY
341/4/0.

Fay and Jimmy Rodolfos Collection.

7 Inch SIMON & HALBIG girl. The bisque head has an open-crown covered with a black mohair wig and is marked:

4/0
DEP
S & H
Germany (in script lettering)

She has brown stationary eyes and two molded and painted upper teeth. The five-piece body is papier mâché and the molded black shoes and blue sox are painted. The author purchased this gem from a doll dealer in 1963 for $20.00. Her value has appreciated many times since then.

14-1/2 Inch French girl with an open mouth and four molded teeth. She has black stationary glass eyes and painted lashes. The open-crown bisque head is a light brown color and is marked (please note the last line of mark was hard to decipher):

23
S F B J
60
PARIS
D / o

The five-piece jointed composition body seems crudely made but it is supposed to be original to the doll. *Wanda Lodwick Collection.*

Above: 14-1/2 Inch girl with a bisque head and a fully-articulated composition body of superior construction that is also jointed at the elbows and the knees. The doll has an open mouth with four teeth and she has pierced ears. The old silk dress is factory made and the printed pattern is old Spanish cigar bands like PRINCIPES and REINAS DE ESPAÑA. The head has an open crown, is a light brown color and carries the markings:

S & C
SIMON & HALBIG
4 1/2

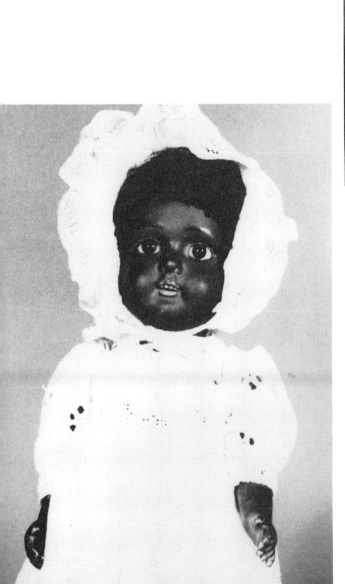

Below: 8-1/4 Inch girl with an open-crown bisque head on a composition body. She has stationary eyes, an open/closed mouth with four painted teeth and a black mohair wig. The head is marked:

Made 41 3
Ex Germany
134

Wanda Lodwick Collection.

Kay Desmonde reports in her *All Color Book of Dolls* that black dolls dressed in African costumes and dolls with features other than European were not sold as souvenirs but were ordinary playthings for children around the turn-of-the-century. The dolls illustrated on the following two pages are examples of this type of doll. They are among the rarest of all black dolls now.

8 Inch all-celluloid baby with Negroid features. The doll has molded curly hair and painted features. The clothing is all original. The doll is marked on the back:

20
FRANCE
(eagle's head symbol drawing)

The Rodolfos Collection

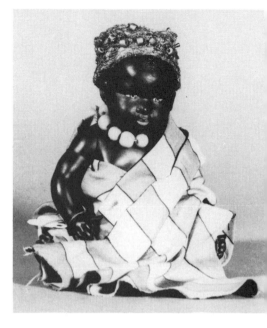

9-1/2 Inch HEUBACH KOPPLESDORF baby on a jointed composition body. The 7-1/2 inch circumference bisque head has sleep eyes and pierced ears and is incised:

HEUBACH KOPPLESDORF
399 13/0 DRGM
GERMANY

The hoop earrings and the straw skirt are original to the doll.

13-1/4 Inch solid-dome head baby on a jointed composition body. He has brown glass sleep eyes and pierced ears and the features are quite Negroid in appearance. The head is marked:

HEUBACH KOPPLESDORF
399-5/0 DRGM
Germany (in script lettering)

Wanda Lodwick Collection.

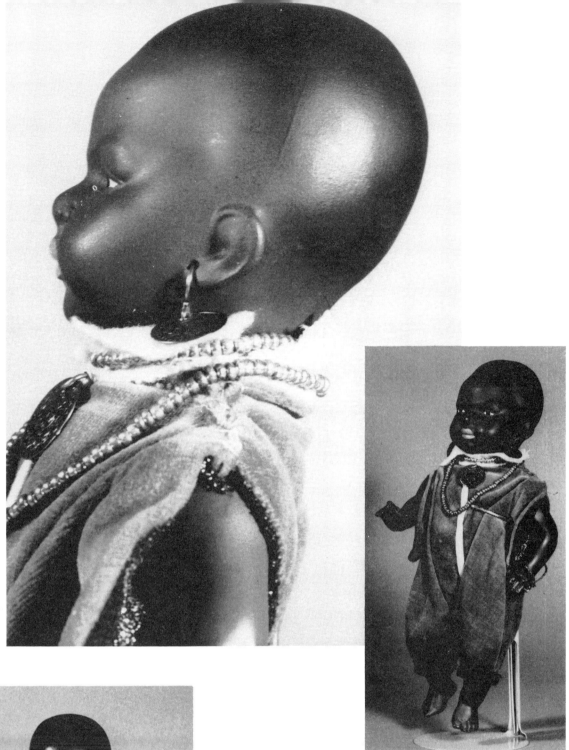

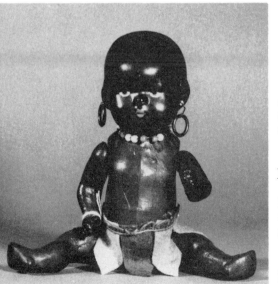

Above Left and Right: 9 Inch painted bisque African with an elongated head. The head and the body are one piece and the doll is marked on the back:

GERMANY
410. 4/0

Each of the four movable bisque limbs is marked: 4/0

Left: 9 Inch all-papier mâché and fully-jointed African baby wearing an original loin cloth of felt. The features are painted and the head is marked:

E 26 S

The Rodolfos Collection.

These small all-bisque black dolls were marketed to sell for a modest cost and were distributed mostly through five-and-ten stores. Some were sold wearing simple costumes and others were sold wearing only diapers or were nude in a cotton bunting.

Left: Most of the little all-bisque black dolls come from Japan, but this 4-1/2 inch baby is incised GERMANY on the back. Only the arms and the curved baby legs are jointed; the features, including the closed mouth, are painted. *The Rodolfos Collection.*

Below: The two girls in crocheted dresses are 5-1/2 inches and are painted bisque with jointed arms and legs only. They have three tufts of yarn hair, painted features and are incised on the back:

MADE IN
OCCUPIED
JAPAN

The boy with painted curly hair is of the same construction and is 6 inches tall. He is marked on the back:

MADE IN
JAPAN

Wanda Lodwick Collection.

Above: The two 4 inch girls riding in the cast iron cart are constructed like the trio on the opposite page. The girl on the left is marked on the back: JAPAN and the girl on the right is marked: MADE IN / JAPAN. The baby in the diaper is 5 inches and is printed on the back in red ink: JAPAN, with 93 incised below. The all-bisque dolls of this type date from the late 1940s. *Wanda Lodwick Collection.*

Above: 2-1/2" Inch unmarked "Frozen Charlie" in china. *Wanda Lodwick Collection.*

Above: 2 Inch fired bisque baby in a "frozen" position. The features are painted and the doll is marked: GERMANY vertically down the back. *The Rodolfos Collection.*

These two pages show black mechanical toy[s] from the collection of Wanda Lodwick. The blac[k] mechanicals frequently presented the black perso[n] in an uncomplimentary light, which many co[n]sidered comical at the time they were sold. In th[e] toy sections of catalogs from the early years of th[e] 20th Century these toys were called *"Musica[l] Negroes,"* (Sears, Roebuck & Co., 1912), *"Dua[l] Negro,"* and "darkies who danced the plantatio[n] breakdown" (Butler Brothers, 1914). Other popu[]lar dancing figures were the "very amusing an[d] fascinating *Alabama Coon Jigger"* (Butler Brother[s] 1914; Sears, 1919) and *"Mammy's Black Boy, wh[o]* shuffles along from side to side" (Montgomer[y] Ward & Co., 1930). Tin toys like these representin[g] the black are no longer made, which makes the[m] very collectible and valuable now.

Left: The man with the bass fiddle has more de[]tailing and is heavier tin than the other mechanical[s] pictured here. When wound with a key, the figure[] measuring 9-1/4 inches high overall, moves h[is] hand to play the fiddle and bobs his head in tim[e] to his playing. This toy probably dates from befor[e] World War I and is stamped underneath:
MADE IN GERMANY

Wanda Lodwick Collection.

Below: *Dare Devil* sits in a cart pulled by a zebr[a] and is about 5 inches high and 7-1/4 inches lon[g] The cart is key-wound and the toy was made i[n] Germany by LEHMANN, a leading producer o[f] mechanical toys prior to World War I. The paten[t] for the Deutsches Reich was 22 January 1907 an[d] the U.S.A. patent was 2 December 1913. All thi[s] information and the company logo are printe[d] around the sides of the cart.

Wanda Lodwick Collection.

ight: The "Dancing Man" is 8-1/2 inches tall and
e wobbles and moves by vibrating at the waist
hen wound with a key. His arms, which would
ave shook as he moved, are missing. He was called
Hey-Hey, the Chicken Snatcher" and was pat-
nted by LOUIS MARX & CO. of New York on
pril 13, 1926, according to the printed informa-
on stamped on the bottom of the feet.

Vanda Lodwick Collection.

elow Right: Shown in profile, this figure is 8
ches tall overall and is from LOUIS MARK &
O. He is key-wound and he carries the uncompli-
entary names *Somstepa* on the sides of the tin
ox upon which he dances and *Coon-Jigger* on the
nds. Sears sold this toy for 67 cents in 1919.

Vanda Lodwick Collection.

elow: The man who dances on a drum when bat-
ery operated is the newest of the five mechanicals,
ating after World War II. The toy is 10-1/2 in-
hes tall overall and the figure moves and bounces
hen activated. The base is stamped:
MADE IN JAPAN

Vanda Lodwick Collection.

The black life-size boy was a store mannequin and is fully articulated for use in displaying children's clothing. He is made of a heavy plaster-composition and is painted in lifelike colors and has glass eyes and a curly caracul wig. Heavy store mannequins of this construction have been replaced by lighter weight plastic models. He measures 30 inches and wears size 18-month clothing.

The dolls pictured on this page are from the *Wanda Lodwick Collection.*

Glass perfume bottle measuring 2-1/4 inches high. Printed across the back in script is:
Germany

The black boy and the elephant are made from wound raffia, the leaves of a palm of the Malagasy Republic which have been tinted in bright colors. The overall measurement is about 10 inches.

The Dolly Sisters are old store stock from the 1930s. They are 2-1/4 inches tall and are made from celluloid with painted features and movable arms only. The clothing is ribbons and is glued on. This set, standing on their original box, is another take-off on the famous Dionne Quintuplets. Each doll is embossed on the back:

JAPAN

Right: The brown celluloid baby boy is 2-3/4 inches tall and is unmarked. His eyes are painted blue and he has no moving parts. These dolls were originally sold in a simple cotton bunting.

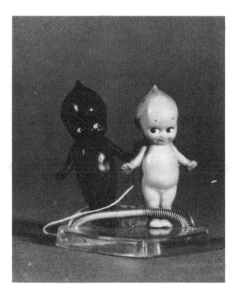

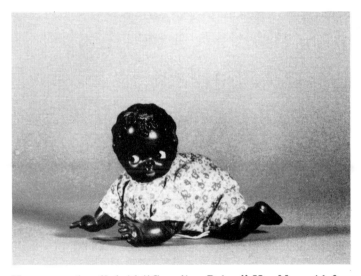

The celluloid Kewpies are 2-1/4 inches tall. The white one has blue wings and movable arms; the black one has white wings on his back and is not jointed. The black Kewpie still carries his ROSE O'NEILL sticker, which is dated 1913. The Rodolfos Collection.

Key-wound celluloid "Crawling Baby." Her Negroid features and her kinky hair are molded and painted, as are the four red bows in the hair. She measures 5-1/4 inches long and wears her original printed cotton rompers. She is embossed on the left foot:

MADE IN JAPAN

The Rodolfos Collection.

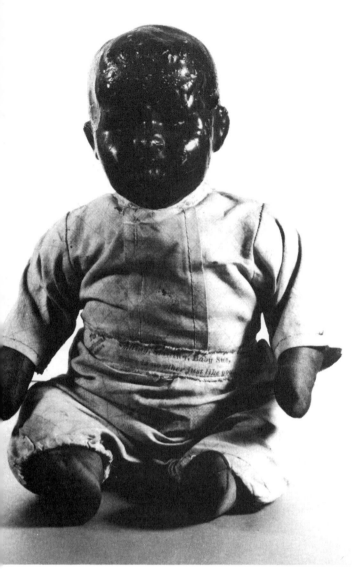

Left: *Baby Sue* has a painted composition head and a cloth, jointed body. She is painted very dark and much of the paint is worn, but the composition is intact although she is from the early years of the 20th Century. The waistband around the front of her original rompers reads: "The Neverbreak Trademark. Smiling, Smiling, Baby Sue, There is no other just like you." *Wanda Lodwick Collection.*

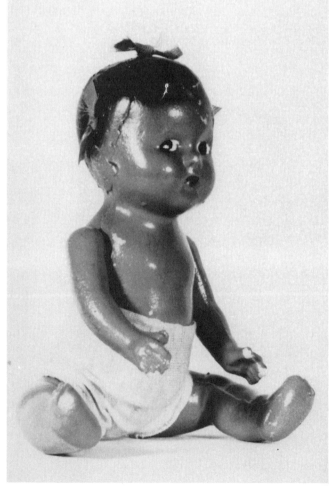

Right: This all-composition baby is unmarked and her original diaper is still stapled onto her body. She is about 7-1/2 inches and is jointed only at the arms and hips. The complexion is painted a light brown; the hair and the eyes are black. She also has three ribbons stapled to her head. This doll is another version of the unauthorized Dionne Quintuplet dolls that are similar to those made by Madame Alexander.

Above: In 1945 Sears & Roebuck sold these brown-colored composition babies for 89 cents each. They were marketed as toys for black children, but were loved as dearly by white children. This tot is 10 inches, has jointed arms and legs, painted features and three mohair pigtails attached through holes drilled in the head. Her simple cotton suit is original. These dolls with molded curls are rather crudely finished and painted so that they would sell cheaply.

Right: In contrast to the above doll, this 9-1/2 inch composition baby is fully jointed, including a swivel head, and is more finely molded and finished although it is of the same general style. The clothing also appears to be original to the doll. The head is marked:

Germany (in script lettering)
1001

The Rodolfos Collection.

Left and Below: *Topsy-Turvy* dolls are two-dolls-in-one from the waist up. From head-to-head this one measures 7 inches. The doll is constructed from composition and both sets of arms are jointed, but only the black head, which has three tufts of string hair, is movable. These same heads were used on the Dionne Quintuplet look-alike dolls and some of them are marked SUPERIOR, a doll company that was based in New York City, although the doll pictured is unmarked. The original dress is a different printed pattern for each end of the doll and the long skirt hides the companion when turned in the opposite direction.

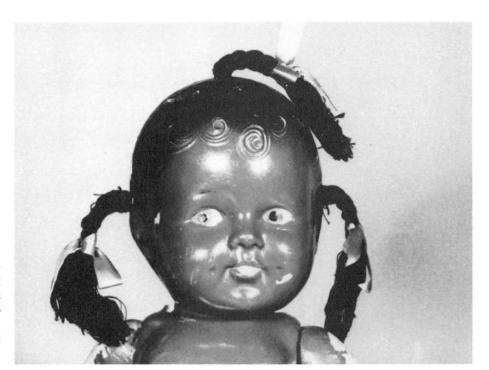

Right: 12-1/2 Inch all-composition and fully-jointed black baby with dimples. She has the usual painted hair and features and three yarn pigtails. She is unmarked. *Wanda Lodwick Collection.*

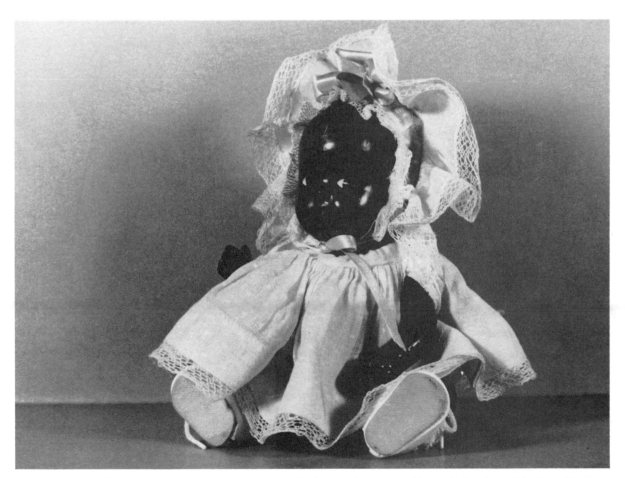

Unmarked 8-1/2 inch all-composition baby with jointed arms and bent baby legs. She is a distinctive example of this sort of doll in that her original clothing is better made and the painted, molded hair is straight rather than curly. (The shoes are replacements.)

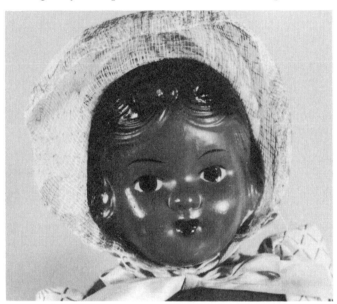

13-1/2 Inch brown girl that uses the same mold as the unmarked Snow White dolls of the early 1940s. She has jointed arms and legs only and painted features. The molded hair is parted in the center and the molded hair bow is painted red. She is completely original and all the clothing is held in place with staples. The doll is made of a grainy composition but she is well painted and finished.

9 Inch unmarked composition girl with jointed arms and legs only. The crude modeling also includes shoes and sox that are painted. The hair is in a Patsy style, which · dates from the early 1930s. *Wanda Lodwick Collection.*

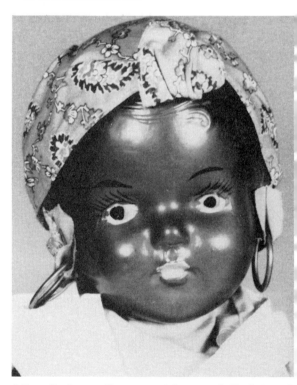

16 Inch all-composition, fully-jointed "Mammy" with painted hair and features. The doll is unmarked and the clothing is stapled in place, as are the hoop earrings. *Wanda Lodwick Collection.*

Right: 10 Inch *Patsy Baby* by EFFAN-BEE in a black version with three tufts of string hair set into the painted hair. She is all composition and fully jointed and has painted side-glancing eyes rather than the sleep eyes that are found on most Patsy Babies of the 1930s and 1940s. The head is marked:

EFFANBEE
PATSY BABY

The back is marked:

EFFANBEE
"PATSY BABY"

The Rodolfos Collection.

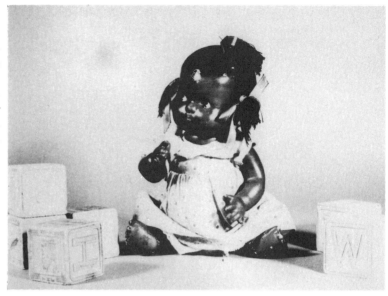

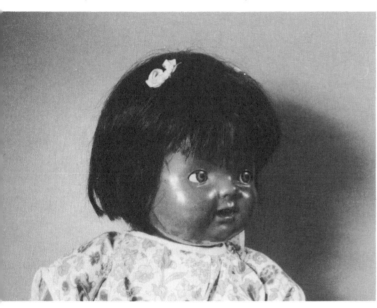

Left: 22 Inch baby with a composition head, half-arms and half-legs, on a stuffed cloth body. The doll is unmarked but she appears to be a HORSMAN. She has dark brown human hair wig, brown tin sleep eyes and an open mouth with two upper teeth. This is a standard white baby doll from the 1930s finished in brown to represent a black child. *Barbara DeVault Collection.*

Right: 21 Inch unmarked girl with a composition shoulder plate head, composition arms and straight composition legs from the knees down. The body is stuffed cotton with a cryer. The face is very similar to that of the Shirley Temple dolls of the 1930s and has brown sleep eyes and an open mouth with teeth and a felt tongue. There is molded, unpainted hair under the wig, which is not original to this doll.

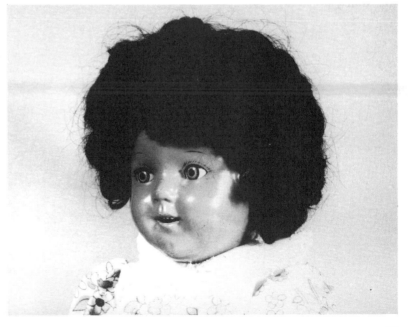

The era of hard plastic dolls (ca. late 1940s to late 1950s) was one in which black dolls were, more than ever, simply the identical mold of a popular, currently produced, white doll finished in a brown color.

Below: This 14 inch *Cynthia* is from MADAME ALEXANDER in 1953. According to the company catalog she also came in sizes of 18 and 22 inches and was described as a walker, although the doll illustrated is not. She is fully jointed, has brown sleep eyes and a black synthetic wig. Cynthia is a very desirable collectible doll today because of her comparative rarity. The doll pictured here is redressed and is marked on the head:

ALEX

Contrast this beautiful p: inch puppets, designed by Austin in 1937 for EFF. with the conventional hard plastic dolls pictu these two pages. The hands and feet of the are constructed from c tion; the bodies are fully and are made of wood, cc with strips of cloth for fle the clothing is all origir

Wanda Lodwick Collectior

The 20-1/2 inch black girl is a "walker," who moves when held by one arm and led across the floor. With each step she turns her head from side-to-side. She is of strong hard plastic and is fully jointed with brown sleep eyes. The construction and the finishing are the same as *Cynthia* on the opposite page except for the open mouth and teeth, but she is unmarked. Her wig and all her clothing have been replaced.

atures are painted and the
the girl is corn rows of
flocking with yarn pig-
oth dolls are of the same
he painting and finishing
ing for the difference in
nce, and the heads are

©
LUCIFER
V. AUSTIN
EFFANBEE

The boy is not marked and is made of the newer type, lighter weight plastic used after the late 1950s. He is 6 inches tall with jointed arms and his sleep eyes have no lashes. The doll was manufactured as an inexpensive toy but has excellent detail in the molded shoes and sox. *Wanda Lodwick Collection.*

The vinyl era (ca. 1950 until the present) has brought us dolls that are perhaps not as aesthetically attractive as earlier dolls. However, the vinyl medium does allow for more subtle detailing and modeling. Generally, the black dolls are also more Negroid in appearance and are a truer representation of black persons, but not always, as it was and still is cheaper to manufacture one basic doll and finish it with the appropriate coloring.

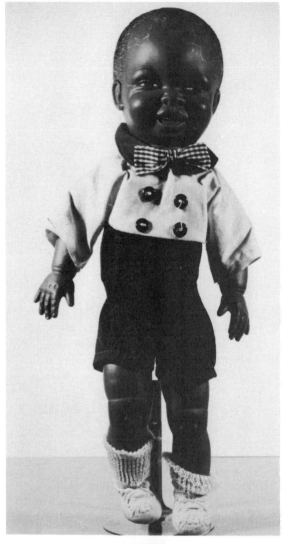

Above: *Amosandra* is 10 inches and is of fully-jointed viny She was designed by Ruth E. Newton, the famous illustrato of children's books. She has painted eyes and painted ha and her mouth is open so that she can nurse. She is marke on the back:

©

COLUMBIA BROADCASTING
SYSTEM, INC.
DESIGNED BY
RUTH E. NEWTON
MFD. BY
THE SUN RUBBER CO.
BARBERTON, O. U.S.A.
PAT. 2118682
PAT. 2160739

Above Left: The all-original 13 inch boy is unmarked and made from the earlier type of vinyl. The soft, cotton fille body is all one piece and the head is also packed with cotto to prevent collapse. The hair, eyes and mouth are painted, a are the four molded teeth.

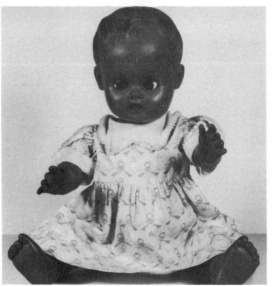

Left: *Sun-Dee* is also from THE SUN RUBBER CO. She 18 inches and is all vinyl, fully jointed and is also an oper mouth nurser. The head is embossed:

SUN-DEE
© SUN RUBBER 1954
MFG BY THE SUN RUBBER CO
BARBERTON, OHIO U.S.A.

Wanda Lodwick Collection.

Above: The 13-1/2 inch fully-jointed vinyl baby from MADAME ALEXANDER is *Baby Ellen.* She has sleep eyes, rooted black hair and is a nurser. The head is marked:
ALEXANDER
19 © 65
The lower back is embossed:
14 F
The tag on the dress reads:
MADAME ALEXANDER
ALL RIGHTS RESERVED
NEW YORK U.S.A.

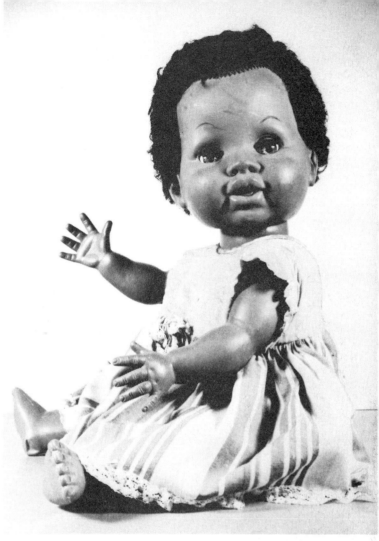

Above Right: 19 Inch girl toddler constructed like the Alexander baby, except that she has a wider nose and fuller lips, which is more typical of a black person. The head is marked:

17
J JOLLY TOYS INC.
T 19 © 69
15

Right: 16 Inch *Tumbling Tomboy* in the black version. She has plastic legs and a plastic torso with a vinyl head and arms. The black hair is rooted and the brown eyes are stationary with extra thick lashes. A plug fits into the right leg at the ankle and a cord is connected to a battery pack that makes her perform her acrobatics. She is marked on the head:
2774
17EYE
S M
E 9
REMCO IND. INC.
19 © 68

Wanda Lodwick Collection.

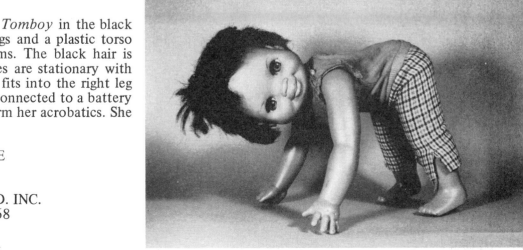

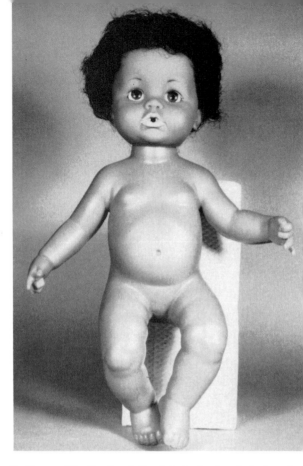

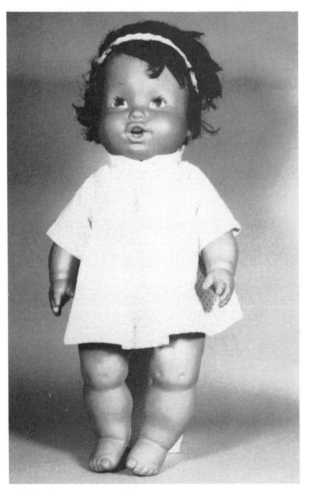

Above Left: 13 Inch fully-jointed vinyl baby by SHINDANA. She has black rooted hair, an open mouth for nursing and painted teeth and eyes. The head is marked:

DIV. OF
OPERATION BOOTSTRAP, INC. USA
© 1968 SHINDANA

Above Right: An open mouth nurser by IDEAL. She has an Afro hairdo of black rooted dynel; the brown eyes are stationary; the vinyl body is all one piece and only the head is jointed. She is 13 inches tall and is marked on the head:

© 1971
IDEAL TOY CORP.
TNT-14-H-194

The body is marked:

© 1971
IDEAL TOY CORP.
TNT-14-B-34
5

Left: 15 Inch *Baby Alive* by KENNER is constructed like the Ideal doll, but she also has a battery compartment in the back so that she can wriggle and squirm like a real baby. She can also pass solid food into her diaper. The head is marked:

3564
2 6 2

KENNER PROD.
19 © 73

Wanda Lodwick Collection.

Above: *Sam and Bessy,* sexed twins who were purchased in Iceland in 1975. They are each 11 inches
tall and are fully-jointed vinyl with black rooted
hair, brown sleep eyes and open mouths. The dolls
are certainly international! The head is marked:

BELGIUM

The arm tag reads:

dvp
MADE IN DENMARK

The original box label reads:

dvp TVILLINGERINE   Sam og Bessy

Right: *Tamu* by SHINDANA. She is 15 inches tall
with a vinyl head, vinyl hands and a stuffed cloth
body. The black hair is rooted; the eyes and other
features are painted. When the string in her side is
pulled she says phrases like, "I'm sleepy." A tag
sewed to the doll reads:

TAMU
© 1970 SHINDANA TOYS
MADE IN HONG KONG

Wanda Lodwick Collection.

Black teen dolls from Wanda Lodwick's Collection:

Above Left: *Talking Christie* from MATTEL is 12 inches tall, has rooted black hair, painted eyes and long eyelashes. The torso is plastic; the rest of the doll is vinyl. Christie is Barbie's "black friend" and is marked on the head:

©1965 MATTEL INC. HONG KONG

The hip is embossed:

© 1967
MATTEL INC.
U.S. & FOREIGN
PAT. PEND.
HONG KONG

Lower Left: *Little Miss Dollikin* by UNEEDA. She is 6-1/2 inches tall, has long rooted black hair and is vinyl with painted features. She is fully jointed, including elbows, waist and knees. This doll also came in a white version and in larger sizes. Her head is embossed:

UNEEDA 1971

The back is marked:

LITTLE MISS
DOLLIKIN R
U. S. PAT.
NO. 3,010,253
OTHER US &
FOR. PAT. PEND.
MADE IN HONG KONG

Above Right: 6-1/2 Inch girl from the Dawn serie by DELUXE TOPPER CORPORATION. She i fully jointed, and also the waist and the knees ben for sitting positions. The head is marked:

4
H 129

The hip is embossed:

© 1970
TOPPER CORP.
HONG KONG
11

Lower Right: 11-1/2 Inch Barbie-type fashion do that is not marked. She has black rooted hair an painted features with no eyelashes.

Reading Counterclockwise:

The *Flatsy* dolls are vinyl and have wires inside for bending them into various positions. The black girl in the picture frame also has a plastic bike and she measures 5 inches. The frame is 8-1/2 by 10-1/2 inches. The package is marked:

© 1968 IDEAL TOY CORP. NO. 0200-6

The Play Time clock measures 7 by 11-1/2 inches and is plastic. The white doll on the pony and the black doll in the cart measure 2-1/4 inches and are bendable vinyl with rooted wigs. The clock is marked:

PRINTED AND MADE IN HONG KONG

The football player is 6-1/2 inches and is vinyl with a plastic torso, constructed like the Deluxe Topper doll on the opposite page. He is marked on the back:

© 1970
TOPPER CORP.
HONG KONG
P

Below: 2 Inch *Kiddle* in original clothing. She has brown rooted hair and painted features. The head is marked:

© M. I.

The back is marked:

©
MATTEL
INC.
HONG KONG

Wanda Lodwick Collection.

63

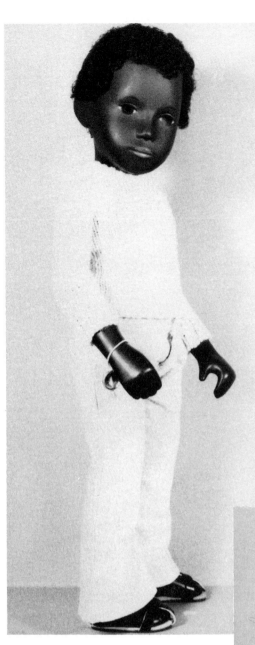

Left: 16 Inch *Caleb* is from CREATIVE PLAYTHINGS. He is constructed of rigid vinyl and is fully jointed and strung. Caleb is one of the Sasha dolls. The white dolls of the series are Sasha and Gregor. The companion of Caleb is Cora. The Sasha dolls were designed by Sasha Morgenthaler of Switzerland and are now produced in England. The doll is all original but he should be wearing suede tennis shoes instead of sandals, which have been replaced from a Gregor clothing set. The dolls are not marked but carry a medal tied to the wrist.

front: reverse:

Below: *The Happy Family* by MATTEL, copyright 1974 They are plastic and vinyl with rooted hair and inset, stationary eyes. Hal is 9-1/2 inches, Hattie is 9 inches and Hon, the baby, is 3 inches. They are all original. The white version of the family is called *The Sunshine Family* and the mother and father dolls are also used for a series of historical American costumes. The American costume series is very popular in Europe but the dolls are produced locally rather than in Hong Kong, as are the dolls manufactured for the American market.

Light: Vinyl *Kewpie* in a 10-1/2 inch black version with a movable head only and painted features. He was dressed in striped pajamas when sold new in the late 1950s and the early 1960s. The head is marked:

1   733/1
CAMEO © JLK

The back is marked:

©
CAMEO

Wanda Lodwick Collection.

Below: *Nancy* by FAMOSA is the Barbie of Spanish dolls. She was introduced in the early 1970s and comes in many, many different versions that vary by hairstyling and hair coloring. Most Nancys have blond hair but she has dark rooted hair in the black and oriental versions. All Nancys have light-colored eyes. She is 16 inches (42 cm) and is fully-jointed vinyl with a twist waist. At last count Nancy had more than 60 complete costume changes and all her own furniture, including closets and dressers for her clothing and her hair pieces. She also comes dressed as *Blanca Nieves,* a Walt Disney Snow White. *Nancy Negra* (Black Nancy) shown here has dark brown hair and green eyes. She is marked on the head:

FAMOSA
MADE IN SPAIN

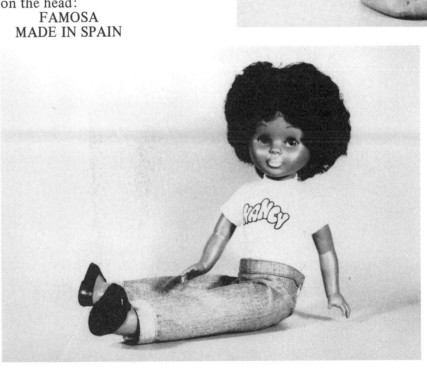

8 Inch girl with painted features, rooted hair, rigid vinyl torso and legs and a vinyl head and arms. The head is marked:

L. ⬠ 5
Reg. Design No.
915/66A
MADE IN HONG KONG

Wanda Lodwick Collection.

All-original *Beautiful Crissy* with her original box. She is 18-1/2 inches tall and has a dial on her back used to lengthen and shorten her long hair. The adjustable hair is set into the center of the head of rooted black hair. Her head is marked:

©1968
IDEAL TOY CORP.
GH-17-Hl20

Her hip is marked:

©1969
IDEAL TOY CORP.
GH-18
U.S. PAT#3,162,976

The box is marked:

© 1970 IDEAL TOY CORP., HOLLIS, N.Y.
No. 1062-9

Lois Barrett Collection.

14-1/2 Inch *Drowsy.* The head, with rooted hair and painted features, is vinyl like the hands; the rest of the doll is stuffed cloth. Drowsy, when the string is pulled to wind the recording mechanism, says such things as, "I wanna a drink of water," and "I wanna stay up." The head is embossed:
© MATTEL INC. 1964

Wanda Lodwick Collection.

Right and Lower Right: Life-size unmarked girl from the early 1960s. She is 35 inches tall and has a vinyl head with black rooted hair and brown sleep eyes. She is unique in that her features are more Negroid than most dolls of this type that represent a black child. The arms are of rigid vinyl and are like the modeling used for the arms of IDEAL'S *Patty Playpal.* The rest of the doll is plastic. She is fully jointed, using the flange method, rather than being strung. All her clothing has been replaced. The Shirley Temple pin was created by Kay Bransky.

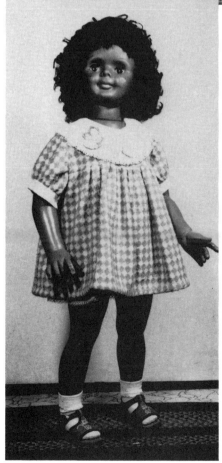

Above: 35 Inch girl by UNEEDA, using the same construction as the above doll. Note how much her facial features differ from the unmarked doll. The head is marked:

U / 24

Wanda Lodwick Collection.

30-1/2 Inch plastic girl with a vinyl head, a rooted Afro hairdo and brown sleep eyes. The head is marked:

© EEGEE CO.
31 E
12

Barbara DeVault Collection.

32 Inch girl of the same type. Dolls similar to this are still on the current market. The head is marked:

EEGEE
©

Wanda Lodwick Collection.

6-1/2 Inch *Rosemary* of the *Rockflowers* series. She has rooted hair in an Afro style; painted features and eyes with no eyelashes. The head is marked:

HONG KONG
© MATTEL
1970

The doll's original box reads:
Their fashions go together!
Make matching groups of three!
© 1970 Mattel, Inc.

Wanda Lodwick Collection.

5 Inch all-vinyl girl with a movable head and arms. She has rooted black hair and painted features, shoes and sox. The back is embossed:

JAPAN

Wanda Lodwick Collection.

9-1/4 Inch *Muhammad Ali,* the heavyweight boxing champion. He was made for MEGO CORP. in Hong Kong and carries a 1976 copyright by Herbert Muhammad Enterprises, Inc. The doll is plastic with a vinyl head and comes with a trigger mechanism that activates the champ's arms so he can "fight" his opponent, a similar black doll.

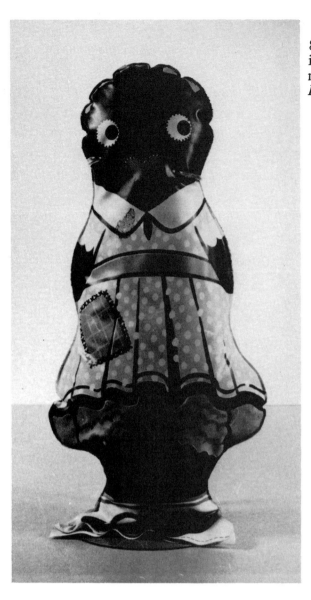

8-3/4 Inch printed and stuffed one-piece vinyl doll that is made like the old-fashioned oil cloth dolls. She is marked DIANA on the back of the feet. *Wanda Lodwick Collection.*

Below: 12-1/2 Inch doll made of cotton-filled silk. She is dressed as an African and has wire in the arms and legs for bending her into various positions. The eyes and the mouth are glued-on felt and all the clothing is sewed into place. Dolls of this type are usually hand-made in Korea. The assembling of them is very tedious and time consuming. The construction, including individual fingers, involves patient and intricate workmanship. *Wanda Lodwick Collection.*

Cotton pillow that was bought as stamped material to be filled and sewed together, forming a doll. The pillow measures 18 inches. *Wanda Lodwick Collection.*

Commercially manufactured cloth doll with jointed arms and legs and painted features. She measures 13 inches and appears to be all original. *Barbara DeVault Collection.*

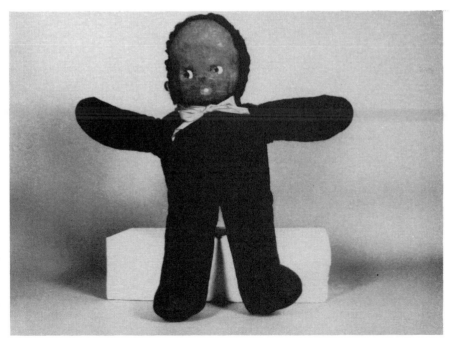

Another commercially manufactured cloth doll of unknown origin. The doll is 12 inches and is all one piece with painted eyes and mouth and a black caracul wig. *Wanda Lodwick Collection.*

These two pages show various types of black dolls in the "Mammy" image.

Above: An electric mixer cover made from a commercial pattern. The upper torso is stuffed cloth; the skirt is used for the covering. The facial features are embroidered. *Wanda Lodwick Collection.*

Below Left: This is a 3-3/4 inch dinner bell covered as a doll. The handle has the facial features painted on. She is a souvenir of Warm Springs Inn in Virginia. *Ted Tarr Collection.*

Below Right: 6 Inch pincushion that appears to be commercially manufactured. She has a painted face, yarn tufts for hair, big hoop earrings and the clothing is sewed in place. *Wanda Lodwick Collection.*

Right: 17 Inch stuffed-cloth, or "rag doll," with the facial features delineated with felt appliques. A tag on the dress reads:
MAMMY
© STUART INC. ST. PAUL, MINN

Below: 6-1/2 Inch stuffed-cloth "Mammy" head with a matching cloth bag for the body. The doll is commercially made and the face has painted features. These items were used to store soiled stockings or linen, or were used as "pajama bags" for children.

8 Inch all cotton "Mammy" with sewed-on clothing. The facial features are glued-on felt circles. The front of the apron is stamped:
New Orleans, La. (in script lettering)

Wanda Lodwick Collection.

73

And from Wanda Lodwick's black doll collection, more souvenir dolls that are caricatures of the black person:

A pair of "Mammys" that are both 13 inches tall. They look like souvenirs of the Bahamas, the self-governed islands in the Caribbean. The dolls, which are all taffeta and fully jointed, wear sewed-on clothing, also made of taffeta. The faces are painted and the doll on the right carries crepe paper flowers in her basket.

These blacks are depicted in the "cotton picker" image from the South. The man is 10 inches and the woman 8-1/2 inches. Both have buttons for eyes and are stuffed cloth. The torso of the "Mammy" is a solid base. The man has raw cotton in his sack.

From the Bahamas or Jamaica: 8 Inch fully jointed, painted-features and all-original woman carrying a basket on her head. The clothing is held in place with straight pins.

Home-made cloth, or rag dolls, created from commerically designed patterns. The couple above is from the collection of Wanda Lodwick; the couple below is from the collection of Barbara DeVault.

Above: 11 Inch boy and girl of jet-black cotton.

Below: 20 Inch boy and girl in brown. The features are appliqued and embroidered; the hair is yarn. The legs, where they are jointed to the body, are stamped "right" and "left." The owner of the dolls considers these twins to be at least 40 years old.

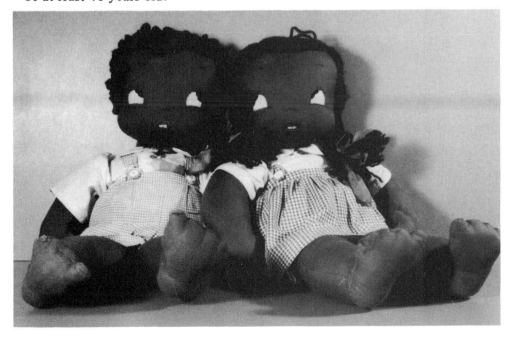

Aunt Jemima advertising premiums with a toaster cover of printed cardboard and cloth. The two plastic shakers on the left are 4 inches tall and are embossed on the bottom:

AUNT JEMIMA
F & F
MOLD & DYE WORKS
DAYTON, OHIO
MADE IN U.S.A.

These items were premiums from Aunt Jemima Pancake Mix, as were the 5-1/2 inch creamer, which is embossed AUNT JEMIMA// REG. U.S. PAT. OFF. on the back, and the 5 inch pepper shaker which is embossed UNCLE MOSE on the back. Both are embossed F & F, etc., on the bottom. *Wanda Lodwick Collection.*

Right: A modern *Golliwog* created and designed by Pam McMillan of Australia. The cloth doll has felt facial features and the hair is black lamb's wool. The doll is 20 inches tall and was inspired by the turn-of-the-century English children's classic *The Adventures of Two Dutch Dolls and a Golliwog* by Florence Upton. *Wanda Lodwick Collection.*

The celebrated black commedian Flip Wilson appeared weekly on his own television show from September 17, 1970 until June 27, 1974 on NBC. The variety program featured various comedy sketches and one of the most popular and most entertaining was when Flip assumed the character of Geraldine.

Original Box

SHINDANA TOYS, a division of Operation Bootstrap, Inc., produced a foam filled cloth doll that is the likeness of Flip on one side and his alter-ego Geraldine on the other. A pull string on the side activates a voice mechanism. Flip says things like, "Easy on that string, I'm only going to tell you one more time!," and "Don't touch me—you don't know me that well!" Geraldine delivers some of her standard lines like, "The Devil made me buy this dress," and "What you see is what you get, honey!" The box is marked:

©1970 Street Corner Productions, Inc.

Skin made in Taiwan

Balance made in U.S.A.

The doll is 15 inches tall and carries a cloth tag with the same information. *Wanda Lodwick Collection.*

Original artist's creations are dolls that are hand-made by very talented doll makers. They are not copies of other dolls or molds taken from popular antique dolls whose value has reached the prohibitive level for most collectors. The dolls pictured on this page are true works of art and are from the collection of Fay and Jimmy Rodolfos.

Carole Bowling calls her creations "needle sculpture." The dolls are made fro tinted stockingette and the facial features are painted with acrylics. The winson black boy and girl are about 9-1/2 inches tall and were made in a limited quanti in 1977. All the clothing is hand-made of typical materials, li real denim for the boy's pants. The wigs are of mohair, with painted additions add to the girl's "corn row" hairdo. The artist has signed her name on the back each doll.

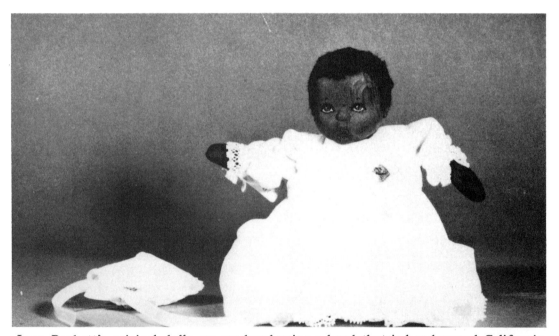

June Beckett's original dolls are rendered using a head that is hand-carved California redwood with flocked hair and a stuffed cloth body. The doll measures about 6-1/2 inches and the head, with painted eyes, also has carved ears and a little round nose. Only six of these dolls were made. The back of the head is marked:

"DIXIE"
by June
'76

The hand-made dress carries a tag that reads: Beckett Originals (in script lettering).

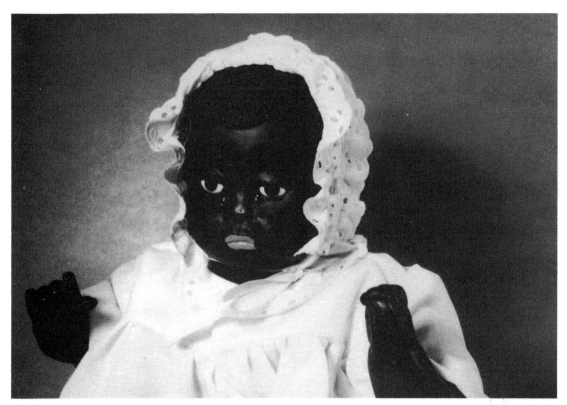

Gail Garver created her interpretation of the Leo Moss Doll that was made around the turn-of-the-century. The head, and the very bent baby arms and legs are made from the artist's own composition formula. The body is brown cloth. The kinky hair is made of the same composition material and was applied separately; the inset eyes are glass with brown irises; tears are running down the baby's face. The doll is very dark in color so the photograph does not do justice to the detailed modeling. The baby is 19 inches tall. *Barbara DeVault Collection.*

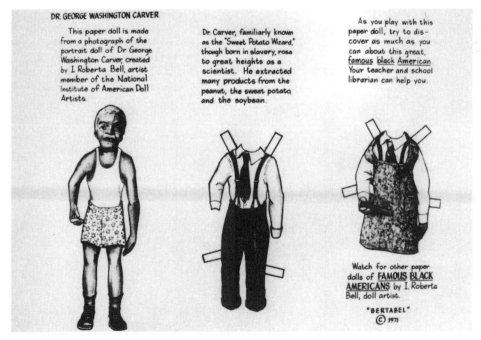

I. Roberta Bell is the artist who drew the original paper doll of Dr. George Washington Carver in 1971. The figure of Dr. Carver measures 5-1/2 inches and is produced in black and white on heavy paper stock. The printed information with the paper doll further explains the artist's intention.

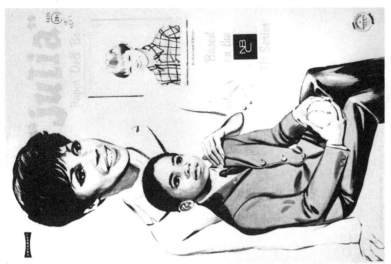

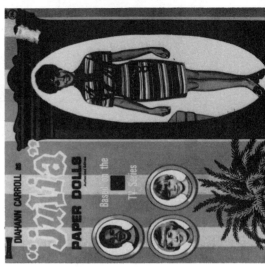

The beautiful and talented singer and actress Diahann Carroll as *Julia* in paper doll form. Julia was a nurse in the NBC television series that ran from September 17, 1968 to May 25, 1971.

Above and Below Right: The booklet at the top is by ARTCRAFT (Saalfield), #4435, copyright 1968; the lower booklet is #5140 from the same company in 1971 and is copyrighted by Twentieth Century-Fox Film Corportation.

Left: Boxed paper doll of *Winking Winny*, #4754 from WHITMAN, copyright 1969 by Remco Industries, Inc.

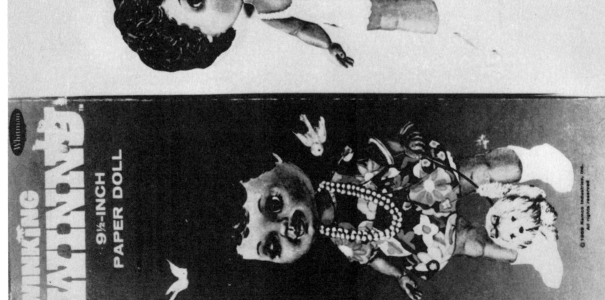

The September 1981 issue of Good Housekeeping had a cartoon story from the "It's All in the Family" series showing the mother and father and the two children at a flea market. The final picture showed the family returning to their car with the father clutching a large bag of puppets. To justify his purchase he said to his wife, "You heard what the man said — 'Howdy-Doodiana is an investment!' I still love Howdy Doody and the gang from "Doodyville" and I will always admit it.

Howdy Doody was one of the first "stars" on television. His show debuted on December 27, 1947, on NBC-TV. "Howdy Doody" was seen until September 24, 1960 totaling 2,543 performances. As a show for children, "Howdy Doody" did not pretend to have any educational value. It was to entertain and children loved it. Howdy Doody himself is now an American folk hero. He and his twin brother, Double, were born in Texas on December 27, 1941, and they lived on a ranch for six years. Then their rich Uncle Doody died and left the twins some property in New York City. Double wanted to remain in Texas but Howdy saw his chance to fulfill his dream of operating a circus. When NBC wanted to purchase Howdy's land for a television studio a deal was made for NBC to construct a circus for Howdy on the grounds. Bob Smith, called Buffalo Bob because he was from Buffalo, was appointed as Howdy's guardian and he helped Howdy operate the circus. Then NBC gave Howdy his own television show and brought in a "Peanut Gallery" of children to enjoy it. The show was about a circus troupe that tried to perform against the wishes of Phineas T. Bluster, a mean old man whose main interest in life was to prevent people from having fun.

Some of the characters on the show were puppets and others were human performers. Clarabell Hornblow, the mute clown, was played by Bob Keeshan (later Captain Kangaroo) and then by Bob Nicholson, followed by Lou Anderson. Among the live performers were also Arlene Dalton as the Story Princess and Judy Tyler as Princess Summerfall-Winterspring. The most important puppets were Howdy, whose voice was supplied by Bob Smith; Phineas T. Bluster, who was 70 years old and "as spry as a pup," Heidi Doody, Howdy's cousin; the Flubadub, the main circus attraction; and Dilly Dally, who could wiggle his ears.

Illustration 2. 25in (63.5cm) and 20in (50.8cm) Howdy Doody dolls by Ideal, circa 1953. Both dolls have hard plastic heads, vinyl spatula-shaped hands and stuffed cloth bodies. They have dark red hair, blue sleep eyes with lashes, mouths with painted teeth that operate with a pull string at the back of the neck and, of course, freckles. The larger doll is on the cover of this magazine; the smaller one is missing some of his accessories. Both are embossed on the neck: "IDEAL DOLL."

Illustration 1. Buffalo Bob with his creation, Howdy Doody, from the cover of TV Guide, June 23, 1953. Buffalo Bob's Howdy Doody had red hair, a big grin and 72 freckles on his face. He is dressed in blue jeans, a plaid work shirt, wore a bandana around his neck and cowboy boots on his feet.

Illustrations 3 and 4. Marionettes by Peter Puppet Playthings, Inc., circa 1950. Above, from left to right: 14½in (36.9cm) *Princess Summerfall-Winterspring,* 17½in (44.5cm) *Howdy Doody* and 15½in (39.4cm) *Clarabell.* Each has a composition head with painted features, moving mouths, composition hands and feet and a flat wooden section for the torso. The Princess also has black yarn braids. No markings. The marionettes were designed by Raye Copelan and copyrighted by Bob Smith. Another version of the *Howdy Doody* marionette is pictured below with his original box.

OPPOSITE PAGE:
Illustration 6. 12 (30.5cm) and 19 (48.3cm) *How Doody* dolls by Eege Both dolls have vir heads with painted fe tures, vinyl hands a stuffed cloth bodi The smaller one has movable mouth and clothing, except for t neckerchief, is part the body. He is Sty # HD 12, made Hong Kong in t 1970s and the markir on the head are oblit ated. The larger doll h a painted molded op mouth with paint teeth and removab clothing and was al made in Hong Ko in the early 197 He is marked on t head: "EEGEE CO ⓒNATIONAL 72 BROADCASTING COMPANY iNC."

ABOVE: Illustration 5. 7¾in (19.8cm) *Howdy Doody* in all hard plastic, maker unknown, circa early 1950s. Fully jointed; dark blue sleep eyes. A lever in the back of the head operates the mouth with its painted teeth.

Illustration 7. Howdy Doody china cup and silver plate spoon with a blue plastic Clarabell pipe for blowing soap bubbles. Only the spoon is marked: "CROWN SILVER PLATE // ©KAGRAN."

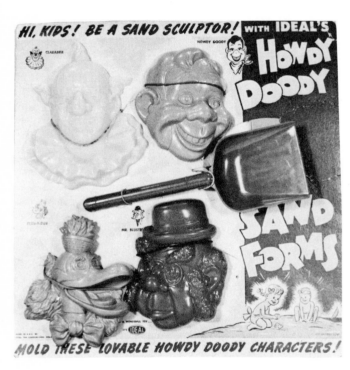

Illustration 8. Howdy Doody "Sand Forms" by Ideal. Clarabell, Howdy Doody, Flub-a-Dub (sic) and Mr. Bluster are each bright plastic. Copyright 1952 by Kagran Corp.

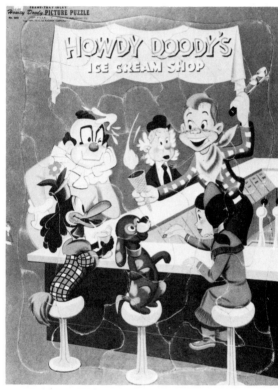

Illustration 9. Howdy Doody Picture Puzzle in a frame by Whitman Publishing Company, No. 2603, 1953 Copyright by Kagran Corporation. At the bottom left is Flubadub, the main circus attraction from the TV program. Flubadub had a dog's ears, a duck's head, a cat's whiskers, a giraffe's neck, a racoon's tail, an elephant's memory and a feather-covered body. H craved meatballs and spaghetti.

Illustration 10. Plastic puppets in different colors by Tee-Vee Toy, Item No. 549, early 1950s. From left to right they are Mr. Bluster, Clarabell, Howdy Doody, Princess Summerfall-Winterspring and Dilly Dally. Each is about 4in (10.2cm) high. A lever in the back of the heads makes the mouths operate, except for Clarabell, who is a whistle.

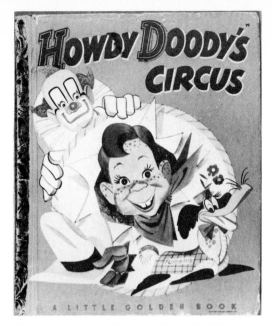

Illustration 11. *Howdy Doody's Circus* by Edward Kean, illustrated by Liz Dauber and Dan Gormley, published by Simon and Schuster, copyright 1950 by Kagran Corporation. This tale tells how Howdy and Clarabell began their circus and encountered the world's only talking Flubadub, who became their ringmaster.

Illustration 13. 26in (66cm) ventriloquist version of *Howdy Doody* by Eegee, 1972. Plastic head with bright red painted hair; painted blue eyes; moving mouth. The hands are vinyl; the body is stuffed cloth. Head marked: "EEGEE // NATIONAL BROADCASTING CO. INC. // 19©72."

Illustration 12. 20in (50.8cm) *Howdy Doody,* circa late 1940s. Composition head and hands; stuffed cloth body. The painted hair is dark red; the mouth does not move and it has painted teeth. The eyes, unlike *Howdy's* own, are brown and have no lashes. The doll is not marked and he is not dressed in original clothing.

Illustration 14. *Howdy Doody* and *Clarabell* from J. C. Penney, Christmas 1977 catalog. Howdy is seen in Illustration 6. The catalog says that both are 19in (48.3cm) tall. Vinyl heads and hands; stuffed cloth bodies.

World Doll's

Elvis Presley ™

In 1983 World Doll, Inc. of Brooklyn, New York, introduced three versions of the Marilyn Monroe doll. For 1984 the success of this series will be overshadowed by the Elvis Presley Collectible Series. Elvis Presley himself was totally original; the celebrity dolls from World Doll maintain this tradition.

COVER: *Supergold Elvis.*

ELVIS' CAREER

MGM Studios in Culver City, California, had the most elaborate and prestigious facilities of all the movie studios. The great stars of MGM, such as Clark Gable, Greta Garbo, Judy Garland, Elizabeth Taylor and many others, had their own private well-appointed dressing rooms at the studio. Only one star ever had two dressing rooms at MGM. That was Elvis Presley. In his lifetime Elvis Presley was the highest paid performer in show business. He also sold more records than any other recording artist.

Elvis Presley was born in Tupelo, Mississippi, on January 8, 1935. In the late 1940s he and his parents moved to Memphis, Tennessee, to improve their financial situation. Elvis got a job as a truck driver. In 1954 he made his first recording for Sun Records in Memphis. Then he came under the management of Colonel Tom Parker who promoted him well and sold him to RCA Records for $35,000, which was the largest recording contract sale up to that time. Elvis' first RCA release, "Heartbreak Hotel," in 1955, made him the greatest sensation in show business.

Presley caused mass hysteria among young people and mass condemnation from older people when he first appeared on television in 1956. His "pelvic gyrations" were considered so terrible that he was only filmed from the waist up for his celebrated guest spots on "The Ed Sullivan Show" because he had disturbed parents and religious leaders with his earlier television performances.

All of Elvis' early recordings for RCA were Number One Hits. Tunes such as "Hound Dog," "Don't Be Cruel," "All Shook Up," and "I Want You, I Need You, I Love You" changed popular music forever. When Elvis was drafted and sent to the army in Germany in 1958, the hit records continued to be released because Parker had anticipated this and had them pre-recorded. It was not until 1967 that Elvis did not have a Top 20 single hit. By 1977, the year of his death, he had sold a record 600 million singles and albums. After Elvis' death the sale of records and albums increased. His fine baritone voice was perfect for all his songs — rock and roll, blues, ballads and country and western.

In 1956 Elvis Presley made his first movie, *Love Me Tender*, a western saga in which he was killed; but because of the outrage of his fans he was brought back at the end to sing another song over the closing credits. Before he went into the army in 1958 he made three more films, of which *Jailhouse Rock* in 1957 is still considered his best. From 1960 to 1969 his career concentrated on the filming of 27 more pictures, all of them tailor-made for his talents. The critics hated these films but his fans loved them and they brought in $15 million at the box office.

Elvis launched a career revitalization in 1968 with a television special that showed that as a stage performer he was better than ever. Then he began concert tours again and smashed all records at Las Vegas. By this time he had become a favorite of "older" fans also. His flashy stage act and his bejeweled costume were imitated by all other performers. Again he began making great recordings like "In the Ghetto," 1969.

At the height of his second career success in 1973 Elvis was divorced by his wife of six years, Priscilla, who retained custody of their only child, Lisa Marie. Then Presley developed health problems compounded with anxieties over gaining weight and loosing his looks. Because of his dependency on an enormous variety of stimulant and depressant pills he died of a minor heart ailment on August 16, 1977.

Because he was so unique Elvis Presley can not be compared to any other performer in the history of show business. After his death his popularity as an entertainer increased. He is still the single most important performer in the history of popular music.

Joyce Christopher completes the final details of the *Elvis Presley* doll, using a metal armature (the post at the doll's back) to hold it securely in position. After the original clay model of a sculpture for a doll is made it is cast in wax. The wax model is the "working model" that is refined and finished before it is electroplated to form the mold from which finished dolls are made. In the wax model stage plastic discs are inserted in the joints to set articulation, the angle of the head and the stance. After this stage no major changes can be made. *Photograph by Paul Christopher.*

JOYCE CHRISTOPHER, SCULPTOR

Joyce Christopher is widely recognized in the doll industry as its best portrait sculptor. Her superb translation of the Marilyn Monroe doll, which was produced by World Doll, Inc. in 1983, further enhanced her reputation. Her latest work for World Doll, the 1984 Elvis Presley doll, is the most original and dramatic portrait celebrity doll produced to date.

World Doll, unlike many commercial doll companies, is proud to give credit to the designer of these portrait dolls, Joyce Christopher. Mrs. Christopher has had wide experience with portrait dolls, and the celebrity dolls that she has created in the past are among the best ever produced.

In the late 1960s she sculpted a small and a large version of Rex Harrison as the lead in the film *Dr. Doolittle* for Mattel. The Rex Harrison renderings are considered by many to be the best portrait dolls created as children's toys up to that time. For Mattel she also did Dick Van Dyke as *Mr. Potts* from the film *Chitty Chitty Bang Bang* and in the late 1970s *Donny* and *Marie Osmond*. The now defunct Shindana Toys produced a series of dolls during the 1970s that were accurate portraits of black celebrities. The best of these was the work of Joyce Christopher. She sculpted the doll versions of O.J. Simpson, Julius (Dr. J) Erving, Jimmy Walker and Marla Gibbs. Joyce considers her best portrait dolls of the 1970s the series of 11¼ inch to 12 inch dolls that she did for Kenner for the *Star Wars* series. Among these were Carrie Fisher as *Princess Leia Organa*, Mark Hamill as *Luke Skywalker* and Harrison Ford as *Han Solo*. For the Knickerbocker Toy Co., Inc. in 1982 she did three versions of Aileen Quinn as *Annie* from the musical film *Annie*.

Portrait dolls are only a part of the creative work that Mrs. Christopher has done for commercial doll manufacturers. Some examples of the items that became successful dolls and toys based upon her sculpture are *Baby First Step, Tippy Toes, Dancerina, Baby Tender Love, Timey Tell, Cynthia,* the 1968 *Ken* head, the 1971 *Barbie* head, and the small *Baby Rosebud* for Mattel; *Precious Penny* and *Hug-a-Bye Baby* for Vogue; *Darcy, Sweetie Face,* the *Strawberry Miniatures,* and the miniature *Care Bears* for Kenner; *Kimberly* for Tomy; and the *Charmkins* for Hasbro.

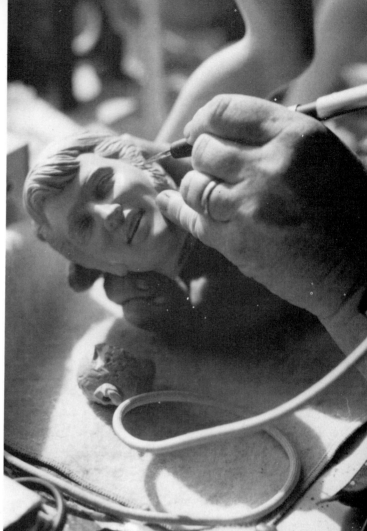

Joyce Christopher adds details to the head of Elvis with a hot waxer. This process is somewhat like modeling jewelry. The waxer adds minute drops of wax for high points and miniature features, such as eyelids, teeth or strands of hair. *Photograph by Paul Christopher.*

Joyce Christopher began sculpting dolls for commercial manufacturers in 1967, at which time she was already a noted sculptress. After she was awarded her BA and MA degrees in art from Scripps College in Claremont, California, she worked as a sculptor on church work and public monuments. Her introduction to portrait sculpture was when she worked for Albert Stewart on a figure of the famous jockey Willie Shoemaker. She also helped to create the horse, *Swaps,* on which Shoemaker is seated, for the sculpture group that is now in Hollywood Park in California. She also worked on monuments in Michigan as a studio assistant for Marshall Fredericks, another sculptor of monumental works, and did illustration work for commercial purposes. Before 1984 the most famous project with which Joyce Christopher had been associated was the doll she did of Marilyn Monroe for World Doll in 1983.

"Elvis is one of the toughest challenges that I ever had," said Joyce Christopher when asked about her most recent assignment for World Doll. "I

spent more time on this doll than on anything I have ever attempted to model. It took me about 800 hours to perfect how he looked when he was at his physical best. I remembered Elvis Presley from my college days, but I became a fan of his when I did the doll for World. I enjoy the demands of portrait work and I become very involved with my projects, and this doll is more special to me than any other I have ever done."

The Elvis Presley project was an exhausting one for Joyce, but the finished doll is the most distinctive portrait doll that has ever been created. The doll of Elvis is portrayed and positioned so that he looks as though he is singing directly to the person who looks at him.

Most dolls are executed in a standing position with the legs parallel and straight down from the torso. The Elvis Presley doll is unique in this respect. His torso is thrust forward in the typical Presley stance and the legs are spread apart and are in the crouching position, a gesture that has been copied by later singers. Yet the vinyl doll is so perfectly balanced that it stands alone.

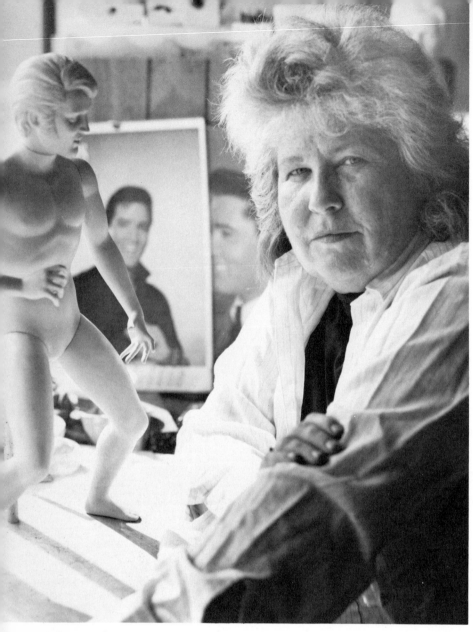

Doll sculptor Joyce Christopher in her studio with the finished wax model of the *Elvis Presley* doll. *Photograph by Paul Christopher.*

understanding of human anatomy cou have created a design which so acc rately captures the essence of Elv magic. Joyce says that the male figure much more difficult to render accurate as a doll than is the female figure. assist her with her design and to achie the correct proportions she employec young model as she prepared to scul the body. Not only did Joyce have have the body correct in proportior but in sculpting a doll the jointing of t arms and legs presents special probler that are not encountered in a so figure. The jointing process also has be engineered in such a way that it w not show under the doll's clothing.

To achieve the stance that w typical of Elvis on stage Joyce spe more time on her original clay model Elvis than she did on any doll that sl has created. She recognized that Elv Presley had great bone structure, but k muscle development was rather mode: To compensate for this she romanticiz her presentation of the torso ar envisioned how the body would loc when clothed and took this into accou in the sculpting. The body of the dress and finished doll does look like Elv Presley in miniature.

Joyce Christopher has admitted agonize over portraits." Her agony a her hours in her studio were worth t finished results. She knew that the har and the body of the Elvis doll were important as the head. She even dic "portrait" of Elvis' hands for the dc Each individual finger is modeled a each hand is open, showing separat fingers, another first for a portrait dc The right arm, which holds a micr phone, swivels at the elbow for po tioning.

In the production of a commerc doll, the translation from the original cl model to a wax model that is refined ar detailed by the artist, and from the wi model to a mass-produced vinyl dc some of the original concept can becor distorted. World Doll takes great care creating production molds that will reta all of the details and nuances that Joy Christopher designed so that the doll v be a true portrait of Elvis, and not jus novelty item, as are so many celebri dolls.

Joyce Christopher's *Elvis Presl* for World Doll is not merely a portri doll. It is a miniature likeness of Elv physical features, and it does "captu the spirit of the man" who became ; American folk legend.

World Doll instructed Joyce, "Capture the entire spirit of the man; don't make just a portrait head." Joyce also knew that if the body were not exciting and almost alive it would not be Elvis.

The vinyl doll from World has sculpted hair. Joyce Christopher has captured this important aspect of Elvis' personality perfectly and shows his thick, dark hair falling over his forehead. Most dolls with sculpted hair, or painted hair, have a hard line to separate the hairline from the forehead. For the Elvis Presley doll, special painting masks were created so that the hairline would be altered, giving it a soft, feathered edge rather than a severe line. This process has given a natural look to the head.

The left side of Elvis' upper lip is lifted in the slight smile he often displayed. Even the minutely sculpted teeth look like Elvis' own did. Joyce Christopher studied thousands of photographs and read many books about Presley to capture his features accurately.

Michael Pietrafesa of World Doll has described the body rendering of the Elvis Presley doll as "expressive sculpture." Only a sculptor with a perfect

THE ELVIS PRESLEY LIMITED EDITION DOLL SERIES

Elvis Presley, the second series of dolls in the Celebrity Collection™ from World Doll, Inc., is a two year numerically limited series that will be issued from February 1, 1984 to January 31, 1986. All of the high standards in portrait doll making set by World Doll in 1983 with the production of the *Marilyn Monroe* doll will be maintained and even surpassed for the Elvis Presley series.

The production of the *Elvis Presley* line carries the endorsement of Graceland, Elvis Presley's home in Memphis, Tennessee, which is now a museum for the memorabilia and the memory of the most important American entertainer of the 20th century. Examples of World Doll's *Elvis Presley* dolls will also be maintained on permanent exhibition at Graceland. The *Elvis Presley Collection* from World Doll is the first license that the Elvis Presley Estate, Elvis Presley Enterprises, Inc., has granted for the manufacture of a doll likeness of Elvis.

The first three dolls from World will depict singing idol Elvis Presley in his prime. All of the dolls will be produced in the United States under carefully controlled standards.

Supergold Elvis

Issue Number One in a series of four vinyl dolls will be limited to 25,000 pieces. This doll stands 18½ inches tall in Elvis' performing stance; at full height it would be 20¾ inches tall.

The simulated white leather jumpsuit is trimmed with gold braid panels in a wheat design; there is a bright red scarf at the open neck; and the doll wears white vinyl boots. Jewelry accessories include a large gold ring on the right hand and a custom-made belt buckle with Elvis Presley's "autograph" and the year 1984 inscribed. The doll is holding a hand microphone of injection molded plastic. The doll's expressive looking eyes are enhanced with a unique two-toned blue iris, something that is seldom done in doll production. Along with a Certificate of Authentication from World Doll, Inc., each of the endorsed vinyl dolls will have the following markings:

Head
J.C. W.D. INC. 1984
Torso —
© 1984 Elvis Presley Enterprises, Inc.
Endorsed by Graceland.

Supergold Elvis seen in front of the outfits considered but not chosen for the final costume design.

Close-up of *Aloha Hawaii Elvis.*

scarves are the only Elvis Presley memorabilia that his estate has released to the public. Each doll will also have a ticket from this last concert, a collector's item in itself.

The Exclusive Edition "Aloha Hawaii Elvis" is presented on a stand in a glass and mirrored oak framed case with an engraved brass nameplate. The nameplate reads:

ELVIS PRESLEY BY WORLD DOLL 1984. ☐

* * * * * *

All of the dolls in the *Elvis Presley Collection* will come with the following credentials that add to their desirability as collectibles:

- A Certificate of Authenticity from World Doll, Inc.
- An endorsement letter from Graceland signed by Jack Soden, the Executive Director.
- A "hang tag" on the doll that includes the collector's registration number from World Doll, Inc.

The Collector Registration Certificate will entitle each collector to be eligible for the contest drawing in which an additional 350 tickets from Elvis' last performance will be distributed to those who have *Elvis Presley* dolls from World Doll, Inc. The Collector Registration and the retail sales receipt are to be returned to World Doll, Inc. by the end of 1984 to insure eligibility for the contest.

* * * * * *

OPPOSITE PAGE: Close-up of *Supergold Elvis* showing accessories: microphone, initialized ring and belt buckle.

PRECEDING PAGE: Close-up of *Gold and Platinum Elvis* wearing a gold lamé suit.

Gold and Platinum Elvis

This special Collector's Edition of *Elvis Presley* is wearing a gold lamé suit. The doll has a porcelain head, hands and legs; the poseable body is constructed of simulated white leather and is from a specially designed multiple-piece pattern. The porcelain head has carefully detailed painting of the hair, eyes and other features. The doll holds a hand microphone. It stands 18 inches tall in Elvis' singing stance; full height is one inch taller. This edition is limited to 4,000 pieces.

Aloha Hawaii Elvis

The *Exclusive Edition Elvis Presley Doll* will compete with World Doll's $6,500.00 *Marilyn Monroe* doll of 1983 that was complete with a custom designed white mink coat and diamond jewelry. This *Elvis* doll is a numbered series of 750 pieces. It is 19½ inches tall, completely made of fine porcelain, and has a jointed swivel waist.

The doll wears Elvis' "Aloha Hawaii" costume that is studded with rhinestones and has a diamond in the belt buckle. Around the neck of each doll there is a miniature silk scarf that was made from scarves from Elvis Presley's own personal wardrobe. The full-size scarves had been packed for Elvis' last appearance — the Market Square Arena in Indianapolis, Indiana, for the June 26, 1977 concert. These

At the front door of Elvis Presley's home, Graceland, in Memphis, Tennessee. From left to right: Jack Soden, Executive Director of Graceland; Robert Seidenberg, Executive Vice President of World Doll, Inc.; and Michael Pietrafesa, Vice President Product Development of World Doll, Inc. *Photograph by World Doll, Inc.*

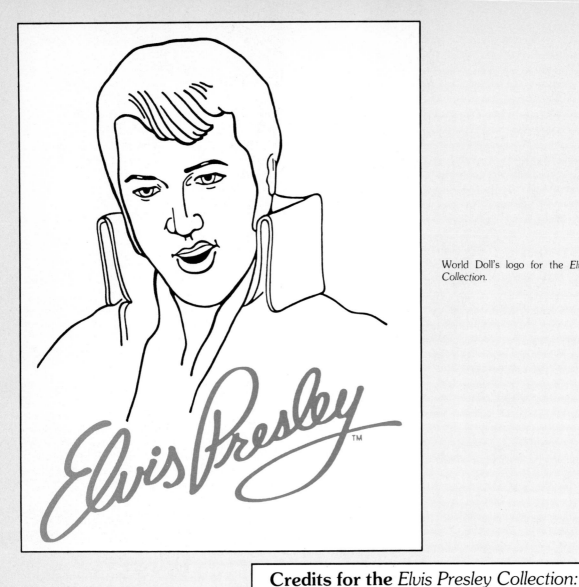

World Doll's logo for the *Elvis Presley Collection.*

Credits for the *Elvis Presley Collection:*

Sculpture	Joyce Christopher
Painting	Joyce Christopher
Costume Design	World Doll Design Group
Package Design	Graphic Horizons, Inc.
Molds	N.E.D. (Vinyl dolls)
	Shader China Doll Co, Inc. (Porcelain dolls)
Stencils	Sprayforms Co. (Vinyl dolls)
Jewelry & Buckle	Arlen Ornament & Finding Co.
Exclusive Edition Aloha Hawaii Costume	
Embroidery and Stonesetting	Jomar Applique, Inc.
Background & Consulting	Graceland Museum
	Elvis Presley Fan Clubs
Public Relations	The Raleigh Group, Ltd.
President of World Doll, Inc.	Steve Strauss
Executive Vice President of World Doll, Inc.	Robert Seidenberg
Vice President Product Development of World Doll, Inc.	Michael Pietrafesa

© 1984 Hobby House Press, Inc., Doll Reader
Cumberland, Maryland

Gold and Platinum Elvis. This special Collectors' Edition of World Doll's Elvis Presley is dressed in a gold lamé jumpsuit. The head, hands and legs are fine porcelain; the body portion of the doll is simulated white leather. Note the specially designed gold medallion over the white turtle neck shirtfront.

The *Phoenix.* Issue Number Two of the Elvis Presley Limited Edition Doll Series. A vinyl doll whose costume is a simulated black leather jumpsuit with a jacket design that captures the essence of the Phoenix. The belt buckle also compliments and conforms with this design.

LEFT AND ABOVE: *Aloha Hawaii Elvis*. The Exclusive Edition Elvis Presley doll is dressed in a fantastic stage costume that features 160 hand-set rhinestones and a 5-point diamond inset in the belt buckle. The silk scarf at the doll's neck is made from one that came from Elvis Presley's own personal wardrobe. Only 750 pieces of this doll will be made.

Issue Number Three of the Elvis Presley Limited Doll Series. As of this printing, World Doll is considering using either one of these specially designed Elvis Presley costumes. At the left is a model called *The Tiger;* at the right is *The Flame*. One of these designs will be the final costume.

Most collections that are built around a famous person, especially in the field of dolls and toys, have as their basis a celebrated individual who became prominent as an entertainer in motion pictures or in some other related profession. There are more types of collectibles of the Dionne Quintuplets than what exists of almost any other famous celebrity. Dionne Quintuplet collectibles are not just mementos of professional careers. Their lives **were** their careers.

The Dionne Quintuplets were internationally famous as soon as news of their birth in Corbeil, Ontario, on May 28, 1934, was rushed around the world. Their popularity has diminished now, as the phenomenon of multiple births is no longer considered a miracle, and as they never went on to accomplish greatness, their fame rests in the past. They are far from forgotten though and the interest that has always been engen-

About The Collectible Dionne Quintuplets

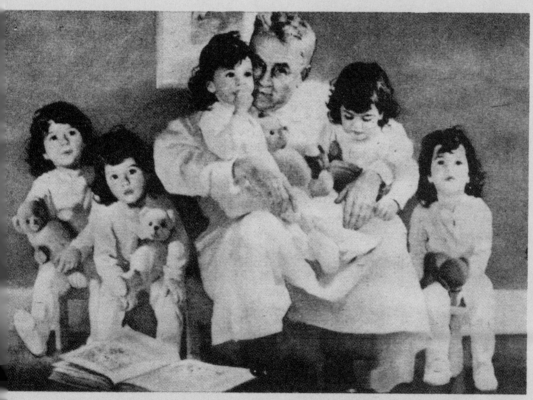

Illustration 1. Dr. Dafoe and the Dionne Quintuplets, painted by Andrew Loomis, who also executed many of the paintings for the calendars and fans depicting the Quints. This is the cover of the paper doll booklet that was free from Palmolive soap in early 1937 if three bands from the product were included with the request. The commercially retailed Dionne Quintuplet paper doll booklets were the following: 1935, Quintuplets: The Dionne Babies, *Merrill Publishing Co.; 1935,* Actual Photographs of the Dionne Quintuplets and Five Paper Dolls *by Queen Holden (dolls are not the Dionnes),* Whitman Publishing Co.; 1936, One of the Dionne Quintuplets *(separate booklets for Yvonne, Annette, Cecile, Emilie and Marie all bearing the same numbers),* Whitman Publishing Co.; 1937, Five Dionne Quintuplets, *Dell Publishing Co.; 1940,* Dionne Quintuplets, *Merrill Publishing Co; and 1940,* Let's Play House with the Dionne Quintuplets *(separate booklets for each Quintuplet),* Merrill Publishing Co.

Illustration 2. 1936 calendar. The Dionne Quintuplets appeared on calendars printed by Brown and Bigelow of St. Paul, Minnesota, from 1936 through 1955. The earliest calendar covers were photographs; the later ones were paintings of the Quints in action, usually depicting a staged or fictional scene.

Illustration 3. Liberty *magazine for June 6, 1936. The cover does not feature the Quintuplets per se, but mention of them would have helped newsstand sales of the issue.*

Illustration 4. The same advertising photographs were used interchangeably for Kre-mel Dessert and Karo syrup. This series of ads highlighted portraits of the different Quints painted by the Hungarian-American artist Willy Pogany. This one is Annette.

dered by everything about their lives is not confined only to the "old-timers" who remember how enormously popular they were in the 1930s. Products and advertising that capitalized on the unprecedented fame of five adorable little girls were mostly distributed in Canada and in the United States, but I have been told by a lady who was confined to a Jewish ghetto in Poland under the Nazi regime that one of the fondest memories of her childhood was when she saw the movies in which the Dionne Quintuplets appeared. Some of the most devoted collectors of Dionne Quintuplet memorabilia were not even alive in 1934 when the world's first surviving set of quintuplets was born.

Many people ask me what prompted me to write a book about the Dionne Quintuplets and how I became interested in them. When I was a small child we had some old spoons whose handles were likenesses of the Quints in the kitchen cabinet so I knew that there were five of them who were all alike but my curiosity did not go much farther. I can remember reading in magazines about the tragedy of Emilie, who died in a convent in 1954, but at the time I did not consider this anything of great interest. It was not until I became acquainted with friends who collected dolls and I discovered that the Quints were also famous as a large series of five

Illustration 5. On the porch of Dafoe Hospital, the Nursery where the Quints lived, February 1938. From left to right: Emilie, Annette, Yvonne, Cecile and Marie.

dentical dolls that my interest was roused.

Collectors of special items are also "buffs" who feel compelled to search out every scrap of information that pertains to their collections. When I learned a little about the real Dionne Quintuplets, it was not enough and I had to discover more about their fantastic childhood. On the surface, it appeared that the Quints led exciting and wonderful lives as children and were visited with tragedies and problems after they grew up. The real story is far more complicated and poignant. Collecting is the route by which I came to learn about the Dionne Quintuplets and the result of what I learned about them is a book, **The Collectible Dionne Quintuplets**, telling of lives that began in a whirlwind of both favorable and adverse publicity and which were affected by villains galore — real and imagined. It was easy to love the Dionne Quintuplets when they were babies because they were beautiful and appealing by any standards of comparison, but understanding what went wrong and why promises were never fulfilled and why dreams were never realized is a problem that would challenge a talented psychologist. The Quints were only ordinary persons but their fame, which out-rivaled that of most internationally prominent contemporary figures, dictated their futures. All of the happiness and the heartbreak that is part of the story of the Quints was not something unique and outside the realm of similar happenings in many persons' lives. However, because there were five of them who were all alike, they could never be considered "normal" and their destinies were bound to be more complicated than those of children who did not live on public display during their formative years.

I have attempted to analyze the lives of the Quints, that seemed so glamourous on the surface, but which affected everyone who played a part in their development, from the midwives who assisted them into the world to high-ranking public officials and their personal doctor who became as famous as they did. I have told of the pilgrimage of tourists who went to Ontario by the thousands in the 1930s to see the five "miracles" for themselves and who could return home with purchases of all sorts of souvenirs, from large framed photographs to the stones and rocks (more "authentic" if purchased from the father of the Quints) that were on the property where they were born. I have gathered and depicted many of the magazines on whose covers the Quints were featured throughout the years and have reported on all the various products that the Quints endorsed to insure sales and which sometimes incited complicated

(and often comical) court cases. I have traced the girls' Hollywood film career, which did not convert them into five identical rivals to Shirley Temple. I have tried to track down and describe the various dolls, games, toys and household accessories that were inspired by the Quints. I have also reported on my own trip to Corbeil where all that remains of the famous Dionne Quintuplets today [1977] is a museum housing almost all the material possessions of their childhood and a lonely cemetery at the end of a cow pasture where Emilie lies buried alone, the symbol of all the unfulfilled promises that the world offered to the Dionne Quintuplets in 1934.

The legend of the Dionne Quintuplets is more than the tragedy of five similar destinies and the listing of all the many collectible items that pertain to them. It is also a commentary on the years of the Great Depression of the 1930s, when life was not as bright for

Illustration 6. In October of 1950, the Dionne Quintuplets visited New York City with their father to take part in a money raising drive for charity. The girls are, from left to right: Annette, Marie, Cecile, Yvonne and Emilie.

most people as it seemed to be for five little girls who became millionaires by virtue of being born at the same time. The Dionne Quintuplets enriched drab ordinary lives at a time when simple forms of pleasure, like being the "fans" of five cute baby girls, were the catalyst that could do this. When prosperity returned with World War II and the Quints lost their babyish charm, the people who had made the five favorites rich, lost interest in them. Now they are history. They did not cause wars nor end wars; they did not establish nations; they did not ever do anything exceptional, but they were certainly something special. □

Illustration 8. *This lamp is an extremely rare Dionne Quintuplet collectible, although it carries no Dionne endorsement. The statuary measures 11in (28cm) high and is 10½in (27cm) across the widest point. The eyes of the babies are painted blue on the chalkware figure and the doctor looks more like Mr. Dionne than it does Dr. Dafoe. On the back of the figure is inscribed: "BREVETE 1934." There were no other sets of "5 Jumelles" (the French equivalent of Quintuplets) to inspire production at the time except the brown-eyed Dionnes. Also marked on the back of the lamp is the following, which signifies at least its place of origin: "PARFUMERIE SOUVENIR// STATION POSTALET//BOITE, 62//MONTREAL."* Jimmy and Fay Rodolfos Collection. Photograph courtesy of Jimmy and Fay Rodolfos.

Illustration 7. *7½in (19cm) all original* Dionne Quintuplet *doll representing* Annette *because of the yellow clothing. The all-composition fully-jointed toddler has the curly molded hair and brown painted eyes. She is marked on the head and the back: "ALEXANDER." This is the marking that is referred to as a marked/unmarked "Dionne Quintuplet" doll because others also carry the name "Dionne."*

The EFFanBEE Doll Company is one of America's oldest doll producers. Bernard E. Fleischaker ("F") and Hugh Baum ("B") formed the company in 1910. EFFanBEE is still producing high quality dolls. All EFFanBEE dolls are collectible but the most loved of all are the ones made in composition. EFFanBEE perfected the "satin smooth" finish for its composition dolls and this look still enchants doll lovers and makes the dolls from the company's "Golden Years" highly sought-after today. The dolls presented here are only a sample of the many outstanding composition dolls from EFFanBEE. Each doll shown is all-original.

Effanbee Composition Dolls

Above: *Baby Dainty*, circa 1924. She is 14½ in. (36.9cm) with a cloth body that has a mama cryer. Her blond mohair wig is over molded hair and she has blue tin sleep eyes with lashes. She wears a yellow organdy dress over matching undergarments and has a matching bonnet. She is incised on the back of the shoulder plate:

EFFANBEE
BABY DAINTY

Right: *Bubbles*, circa 1925. Bubbles was the first big seller for EFFanBEE and she came in many sizes. This one is 16 in. (40.6cm) and has a cloth body with a cryer inside. She has yellow sprayed hair, blue tin sleep eyes, an open mouth with two upper teeth and a tongue. The white organdy dress is labeled: EFFanBEE// BUBBLES // REG. U.S. PAT. OFF. The back of the shoulder plate is embossed:

EFFANBEE
DOLLS
WALK - TALK - SLEEP
MADE IN U.S.A.

Patsyette Texas Ranger, 1936. Like all Patsyettes, the doll is 9½ in. (24.2cm) tall. She has painted red hair and the unusual painted blue eyes. Her outfit is red and white checked cotton. The felt hat has a round label reading: TEXAS // 1936 // CENTENNIAL. She is marked on the shoulders:

EFFANBEE
PATSYETTE
DOLL

Charlie McCarthy, circa 1938. He is 15¼ in. (38.7cm) tall with painted brown hair and eyes. A pull string through the back of the head makes him "talk." He is on a cloth body and wears a navy blue felt blazer with white felt pants. The shoes are composition. He is marked on the back of the shoulder plate:

EDGAR BERGEN
CHARLIE McCARTHY
AN
EFFANBEE PRODUCT

Patsy Tinyette Toddlers in Tyrolean costumes, circa late 1930s. They are 7¾ in. (19.8cm) tall. The boy's painted eyes are brown; the girl's are blue. The round buttons are from White Horse Inn, a gift shop, where they were purchased. The shoulders are marked:

EFFANBEE
BABY TINYETTE

Snow White, circa 1939. This variation of the Anne Shirley doll is 14½ in. (36.9cm) tall with an open mouth and four teeth, a blond human hair wig and green sleep eyes. The dress is pink taffeta trimmed in maroon. Her paper tag cites that she is "Snow White from Grimm's Fairy Tales." Her head is embossed EFFANBEE and the back is embossed:

EFFANBEE
ANNE-SHIRLEY

Patsy Ann, circa 1930. Patsy Ann is 19 in. (48.3cm) tall. This version has brown glass sleep eyes and a brown human hair wig. Her pleated organdy dress is labeled and she wears her EFFanBEE heart bracelet. She is marked across the shoulders:

EFFANBEE
"PATSY-ANN"
©
PAT. #1283558

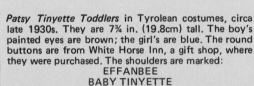

and George Washington Patsyettes. They have white mohair and brown painted eyes. The clothing is organdy and felt. These were sold as souvenirs at Mount Vernon in the 1930s and the

Little Lady from the World War II years. She is 17½ in. (44.5cm) tall with brown sleep eyes. Due to scarcities of essential materials her wig is yellow yarn. The original box says that she is style #8500. She wears a long taffeta gown. The head and back are marked: EFFANBEE U.S.A.

Left:
Little Lady Gibson Girl from the 1940s. At 27 in. (68.6cm) she is the largest Anne Shirley/Little Lady doll. She has brown sleep eyes and a dark brown human hair wig. The blouse is white organdy and the skirt and matching umbrella are taffeta. Only the head is marked: EFFANBEE.

Right:
Anne Shirley, circa early 1940s. This 15 in. (38.1 cm) Flower Girl from a wedding party series wears a pink net dress over pink taffeta with matching pantaloons. She has a blond human hair wig and blue sleep eyes. The head is unmarked; the back is marked:
EFFANBEE
ANNE-SHIRLEY

103

Left: *Suzanne*
from the early 1940s.
She is 13½ in. (34.3cm)
tall with brown sleep eyes
and a dark blond mohair wig.
The sheer white gown is trimmed
in black lace. The back is marked:
SUZANNE
EFFANBEE
MADE IN
USA
Right: *Kewpie*, 1948. The 13 in. (33cm)
fully-jointed Kewpie is No. 9713 in the 1948
EFFanBEE catalog wearing this sunsuit. The doll is
described as "The original Rose O'Neill 'Kewpie'
Doll/a Cameo Doll Product." This doll is not marked.
Middle: *Candy Kid Champ,* 1948. He is 13 in.
(33cm) tall with painted brown hair and blue sleep
eyes. The boxing gloves are real leather. This is one
of the very last composition dolls from EFFanBEE.
Both the head and back are embossed: EFFANBEE.

Effanbee's *Patsy Ann* with four *Patsyettes*, all wearing original costumes.

THE PINOCCHIO ERA

Illustration 1. 12in (30.5cm) *Pinocchio* by Crown Toy Manufacturing Company, 1939. All-composition and fully-jointed. Blue painted eyes; black molded and painted hair. The head is marked: d NICCHIO // W. DISNEY. PROD // C.T." The "Pinocchio Express" is No. 720 by Fisher Price Toys, 1939. It is a wooden pull toy that makes a "clickety-clack" sound when the axle from the back wheels hits a metal bar. The picture of Pinocchio and the pictures on the sides of the cart are lithographed on enameled paper and applied.

During Christmas week of 1937 the first feature length fully-animated Walt Disney film *Snow White and the Seven Dwarfs* was released. It was a smashing success. Some doll and toy manufacturers like Ideal, Alexander and Knickerbocker had already applied for the rights to produce merchandise that would tie in with the film. Most of the products related to Snow White were manufactured and sold after the movie was released. In February of 1940 *Pinocchio*, Disney's second fully-animated feature was released. This time the sales potential of tie-in products was realized in advance and by the summer of 1939 dozens of products had been designed and could be ordered by wholesalers and retailers. Kay Kamen Ltd., a business firm operated in New York City by Mr. Kay Kamen, represented Walt Disney Productions in licensing all merchandise based on characters in the film. Disney items had become such big business that Kay Kamen Ltd. printed the *Walt Disney Character Merchandise Catalogue* for retail buyers. For 1940 to 1941 Pinocchio was still the featured product.

Pinocchio originated in 1880 in Italy when journalist Carlo Lorenzini,

who was born in Florence in 1826, needed money. He decided to write for children and the first chapter of *Pinocchio* was printed in a children's journal. Pinocchio's adventures were told in 37 installments. The tale was later published in book form in more than 80 languages, including at least 100 English editions. Lorenzini, as the author of *Pinocchio,* used the name Carlo Collodi. Collodi, Italy was the town where he grew up. In September of 1981 a festival was held in Collodi to celebrate the centenary of *Pinocchio,* the greatest Italian children's classic.

Pinocchio is basically a retelling of the parable of "The Prodigal Son" from the *New Testament* of the Bible. Pinocchio was a puppet who was given the chance to become mortal. He ran away from his creator/father Geppetto, fell into bad company, had all sorts of risks to his life and in the end reformed and was forgiven. His reward was that he became a real boy at last, and that he had a human soul.

The Disney version of *Pinocchio* gave more life and character to the principals. It also emphasized the fact that Pinocchio's nose would grow long when he told lies and brought out the

point that good can triumph over ev[il]. *Pinocchio* is now considered Disne[y's] masterpiece of all of his fully-animat[ed] films. In 1940 it was not really su[c]cessful at the box office but with [all] its re-issues it has become a popul[ar] classic of the genre. The movie do[es] not follow the original story [line] sequence. In the film the Blue Fai[ry] appeared at the beginning, where[as] in the book she did not come alo[ng] until the 16th chapter to appoint [a] Crow, a Screech-Owl and a Talki[ng] Cricket to prevent Pinocchio fro[m] becoming "a scamp, a rogue, a vag[a]bond." In the film the Talking Crick[et] was Jiminy Cricket and he usurp[ed] the functions of the Crow, th[e] Screech-Owl and even Pinocchio hi[m]self and acted as Pinocchio's co[n]science. The Fox and the Cat, th[e] villains, were called J. Worthingt[on] Foulfellow and Gideon. Other cha[r]acters were also given names by Disn[ey] for the movie. The worst villain w[as] Stromboli, the puppet master; th[e] Goldfish was Cleo and the Dog-Fi[sh] or the Monster was Monstro the wha[le]. The film also included songs, like th[e] theme song "When You Wish Upon [a] Star" composed by Leigh Harline wi[th] lyrics by Ned Washington. Som[e] critics at the time the film was releas[ed] accused it of being too violent a[nd] frightening for children, but compar[ed] to the original version by Collodi [it] was rather restrained.

The doll and toy versions [of] Pinocchio and all the pictures [of] Pinocchio that appear on other iter[ms] that are copyrighted by Disney are th[e] creation of animators Frank Thoma[s,] Milt Kahl and Ollie Johnston. The[y] constructed a wooden model [of] Pinocchio to guide the artists a[nd] animators. The Disney dolls a[nd] other items are still very similar [to] the original model. The United Stat[es] trademark "Pinocchio" was appli[ed] for in June of 1939 to protect th[e] design. Geppetto's Pinocchio from th[e] Collodi story was more like th[e] elongated Pinocchio dolls and figur[es] that are still imported from Europ[e] and none are as cute as the Disne[y] version.

The Walt Disney Pinocchio E[ra] began in August of 1939 when the do[ll] and toy market was blitzed with adve[r]tisements for Pinocchio merchandis[e.] Kay Kamen Ltd. helped to emphasi[ze] that Walt Disney Productions was th[e] creator and the owner of all rights [to] the characters from the motio[n] picture *Pinocchio.* Retailers we[re] warned to look for the copyrig[ht] notice on all Pinocchio merchandi[se] and if any infringements were mark[et]ed both the manufacturer of th[e] merchandise and the retailer would b[e]

ld liable in court. Kay Kamen Ltd.
omised merchants that orders would
ur in "from all points" and that
ey should "profit by the 'Snow
hite' experience and place bigger
d more complete initial orders than
ey would have considered when
now White' was introduced." Manu-
cturers who wished to supply part
the expected demand were advised
apply promptly to the Kamen
fice to secure rights for Pinocchio
ms.

The following describes the
oducts of the manufacturers who
d applied for a license to produce
erchandise based on Walt Disney's
nocchio before the film was released
1940. (They are listed in alpha-
etical order.) I consider these
nocchio collectibles the most desir-
le of all that have ever been pro-
ced. *Playthings* magazine was a
luable aid in compiling this infor-
ation.

J. C. BLAIR COMPANY, Hunt-
ingdon, Pennsylvania. Tablets and
school stationery.
GEORGE BORGFELDT & COM-
PANY. Wooden figures, dolls,
toys, tea sets and other items.
Borgfeldt's *Walking Pinocchio* was

No. 950   No. 5035   No. 475   No. 1000   No. 450   No. 550

Illustration 2. Crown Toy Manufacturing Co. advertisement from *Playthings,* January 1940.

tration 3. 16in (40.6cm) *Pinocchio* and
 (30.5cm) *Jiminy Cricket* by Knicker-
ker Toy Co., Inc., 1939. *Pinocchio* is all-
position and fully-jointed with painted
 eyes and painted black hair. *Jiminy* is
ted at the head and at the arms and is also
position. *Shirley's Dollhouse.*

about 10in (25.4cm) and was all-
composition with painted clothing. A key-wind mechanism made
the legs move so the doll could
"walk." The item retailed for
$1.00
3. MILTON BRADLEY COMPANY.
Games. Walt Disney's Pinocchio
Game box and game board
depict scenes from the film.
4. BRYANT ELECTRIC COM-
PANY. Beetleware dishes and
tableware.
5. CRAMER-TOBIAS-MEYER, INC.
Give-away booklets, advertising
statement enclosures and other
items.
6. CROWN TOY MANUFACTUR-
ING COMPANY, Brooklyn, New

York. Dolls and banks.
Dolls:
1. Painted composition head
Pinocchio "Glove Doll" with
simple cloth glove portion,
No. 35. Retailed for 25¢.
2. Painted composition head
Pinocchio "Glove Doll" with
glove portion that wore a suit
and tie, No. 5035. Retailed
for 50¢.
3. 9½in (24.2cm) *Pinocchio*
doll, No. 950. All-composition; jointed only at the
arms; painted features and
clothing. Retail was 50¢.
4. 8-3/8in (21.2cm) *Pinocchio*
doll, No. 550. (Later called

Illustration 4. 7½in (19.1cm) *Pinocchio* by Ideal, 1939. Composition head; wooden body in jointed sections. The collar is white oilcloth and the bow tie is blue felt.

Illustration 5. Tin toy, "Pinocchio the Acrobat" by Louis Marx and Company, 1939. The base measures 11½in (28.6cm) long; the over-all height is 16½in (41.9cm); and the figure of Pinocchio is 7in (17.8cm). The item is marked with the Marx logo and is copyrighted by Walt Disney Productions. *Shirley's Dollhouse.*

Illustration 6. Pinocchio Valentines by Paper Novelty Mfg. Co., 1939 (for the 1940 market

No. 500.) All composition; jointed only at the arms; painted features with cloth clothing, including the hat. Retail was 75¢.

5. 12in (30.5cm) *Pinocchio* doll, No. 1000. (Later called No. 1010.) All-composition and fully-jointed with cloth clothing, including hat. Retail was $1.00.

6. 15in (38.1cm) *Pinocchio* doll, No. 152/15. All-cloth. Retail was $1.00

7. 15in (38.1cm) *Jiminy Cricket* doll, No. 160/15. All-cloth. Retail was $1.00.

Banks:

1. About 5in (12.7cm) Pinocchio, No. 450. All-composition. The figure leans against a tree trunk. Retail 25¢.

2. 7in (17.8cm) Pinocchio, No. 475. All-composition. Pinocchio is seated. Retail 50¢.

3. 6in (15.2cm) Jiminy Cricket, No. 480. All-composition. Retail was 25¢.

Crown Toys carried the most extensive advertising for Pinocchio items in *Playthings* in 1939. The company invited retailers to "write for sample assortment."

7. DeWARD NOVELTY COM PANY. Ring Toss Toy.

8. JOSEPH DIXON CRICIBL COMPANY. Pencils, pencil boxe and pencil pouches.

9. A. S. FISHBACH, INC. Masque ade costumes. Costumes and mas sets of Pinocchio, Jiminy Cricke the Blue Fairy, J. Worthingto Foulfellow and Figaro. Reta price was from $1.00 to $10.0 per set.

10. FISHER PRICE TOYS, INC East Aurora, New York. Toys Wooden pull toys with decorate lithographed pictures. One wa Pinocchio riding a donkey, who when pulled, caused Pinocchio t strike a bell on the donkey' head. Another was the "Pinocchi Express," in which Pinocchi pedals an open cart that can hol various toys. When these toy are pulled a piece of metal that i hit by the back wheel axle make a sharp "clickety-clack" sound.

11. FULTON SPECIALTY COM PANY, Elizabeth, New Jersey Rubber stamp sets. These set included outline stamps in re rubber, a washable inked stam pad, a pad of paper and a set o crayons. The smaller set retaile for 25¢. A larger set that als

Illustration 7. 5in (12.7cm) Geppetto figure by Multi Products, Chicago, date unknown but probably 1950s. Geppetto is brightly painted and is made of pressed fibre.

included four scenes from the movie to stamp and color retailed for $1.00.

12. **GROSSETT & DUNLAP, INC.** Books.

13. **N. H. HILL BRASS COMPANY,** East Hampton, Connecticut. Metal pull and bell toys. These were pull toys. There were examples of Pinocchio shaking a bell at Figaro; Cleo bobbing up and down in a transparent tank and swimming towards a seated Pinocchio who was shaking a bell; a dump cart with chimes; and another chime toy that depicted Pinocchio and Jiminy.

14. **IDEAL NOVELTY & TOY COMPANY.** Composition and stuffed dolls. Dolls with composition heads and jointed wood segment bodies:
  1. 7½in (19.1cm) *Pinocchio* with a molded painted hat, oilcloth collar and felt bow tie. Retail was $1.00.
  2. 10½in (26.7cm) *Pinocchio* with a ribbon bow tie and a felt hat. Retail was $1.50.
  3. 21in (53.3cm) *Pinocchio* with the same construction.
  4. 8½in (21.7cm) *Jiminy Cricket* made from wood segments, including a wooden head. Felt brim on the hat;

felt collar; ribbon necktie. He also carries a wooden umbrella.

15. **KNAPP ELECTRIC COMPANY, INC.** Wooden toys and electric questioner. A wood construction "Walt Disney's Pinocchio Toy Set" retailed at $1.50. The characters included Pinocchio, Jiminy Cricket, Figaro, Cleo and Donkey. The various parts, when assembled, formed figures with flexible joints that assumed all manner of "natural or absurd poses." (These were similar to Knapp's popular "Krazy Ikes.") The "Electric Questioner" listed at $3.00.

16. **KNICKERBOCKER TOY COMPANY.** Dolls. *Pinocchio* was in composition or stuffed cloth from 11in (27.9cm) to 36in (91.4cm) and retailed from $1.00 to $15.00. *Jiminy Cricket* was made

ABOVE: **Illustration 8.** 11in (27.9cm) *Pinocchio* by Effanbee, No. 1192, 1981. This is *NOT* a Disney Pinocchio. He has a vinyl head and arms and a plastic torso and legs; rooted reddish-brown hair; blue sleep eyes with molded lashes; bright red painted nose. The head is marked: "EFFANBEE // © 1975 // 1176."

RIGHT: **Illustration 10.** 8½in (21.6cm) *Pinocchio* from Germany, a Carl Original, a current product. Vinyl head and arms; plastic body and legs. The wig is black plush; the painted eyes are blue. He has two unusual features: The nose "grows" by pulling it to make it longer and a key-wind mechanism makes him "walk." This is *NOT* a Walt Disney design.

Illustration 9. 10in (25.4cm) *Pinocchio,* a marionette by Pelham Puppets, circa 1967. Ceramic composition head and feet; plastic hands, arms and legs. Painted brown eyes. This is *NOT* a Disney design, although it is very close. It is sometimes advertised as Disney, but is not marked as such. Made in England.

Illustration 11. 10¼in (26.1cm) *Jiminy Cricket* that was made in Italy, a current product. All-vinyl and jointed at the head and arms. Copyrighted by Walt Disney Productions.

in three sizes in composition and stuffed cloth and retailed from $1.00 and up. There was also a line of figurines of the characters from *Pinocchio* measuring 3in (7.6cm). Ads in 1939 told of dolls of other characters — Figaro the Cat, Donkey and Cleo the Gold Fish (sic). All-composition dolls from Knickerbocker:

1. 10in (25.4cm) *Pinocchio* with a jointed head and jointed

Illustration 12. Hand puppet, or glove puppet of *Pinocchio* from an unknown manufacturer, 1960s. Vinyl head with painted features; cotton glove portion. Copyright by Walt Disney Productions and made in Japan.

arms. He wears cloth clothing and a hat and has painted shoes.
2. 14in (35.6cm) *Pinocchio* that is fully-jointed. He wears cloth clothing, a cloth hat and felt shoes.
3. 12in (30.5cm) *Jiminy Cricket.* Fully-jointed. He wears felt clothing and a felt hat.

17. RICHARD G. KRUEGER, INC. Dolls. (I have never seen any Pinocchio dolls from this company.)
18. LOUIS MARX & COMPANY. Mechanical toys. These are lithographed tin toys. Various jointed figures of Pinocchio perform acrobatic stunts, for example.
19. OAK RUBBER COMPANY, Ravenna, Ohio. Rubber balloons and inflatable rubber toys. A red, white and blue inflatable Pinocchio figure came in sizes of 10¾in (27.4cm) and 18in (45.7cm).
20. OHIO ART COMPANY. Lithographed metal toys, tops, sand pails, sand sets, sprinklers, musical toys, tea sets, drums, laundry sets and carpet sweepers.
21. OLD KING COLE, INC. Window and department store displays.
22. PAAS DYE COMPANY. Easter egg decorations. Retailers could order a display unit that included a Knickerbocker Pinocchio doll and five wire display racks for the packages of Easter egg dye. There were 100 assorted packages of egg dye, featuring Disney Characters and concentrating on Pinocchio. The packages sold for 10¢ each or three for 25¢. Retailers were told that they could promote sales by making "Pinocchio the center of their Easter display and cash in on his nation-wide popularity by offering him (the doll) as a prize for the most beautifully decorated Easter Egg. Good

will and enjoyment of far reaching publicity should result with a minimum of effort and increase sales in egg dyes and other Easter items as well."
23. PAPER NOVELTY COMPANY. Valentines. There were at least 12 different designs for the "Double-Glo" valentine line "in all price ranges."
24. PARKER BROS., INC. Games. One game was printed in two colors and it retailed for $1.00. The other was a party game called "Pin the Nose on Pinocchio" and it also retailed for $1.00.
25. PLASTIC NOVELTIES, INC. Catalin pencil sharpeners.
26. RANDOM HOUSE, INC. Books.
27. R.C.A. VICTOR CORP. Phonograph records.
28. SEIBERLING LATEX PRODUCTS COMPANY, Akron, Ohio. Rubber toys and figures. This company was always among the first to have Walt Disney toys ready for the retail market. Seiberling's stand-up rubber figures had noise makers inside and retailed for 25¢. They were 6in (15.2cm) in height and included Pinocchio, Jiminy Cricket, Figaro the Cat, Cleo the Goldfish and the Donkey. Inflated and sponge rubber play balls had Pinocchio characters printed on them.
29. THORENS, INC. Music boxes.
30. WHITMAN PUBLISHING COMPANY. Books and games.
31. WORLD TOY MFG. CORP. Dolls. This company was famous for its "World Animals," a line of novelty stuffed toys. In 1940 it advertised a cloth Pinocchio in "three sizes and styles, standing or sitting" to retail for $1.00, $1.50 and $2.00.

Illustration 13. Pinocchio and Jiminy Cricket by Matchbox, 1979. The figures are plastic; the car and truck are die-cast metal. Copyright by Walt Disney Productions. Matchbox is a trademark of Lesney Products & Co., Ltd., of London, England. Made in Hong Kong.

Collectible Patsy Dolls
and Patsy-Types

Introduction

The Fleischaker & Baum Doll Company, known by its rounded-out initials "Eff-an-bee," in 1928 introduced a trend-setting doll that has become possibly the most famous American doll of all time outside of the celebrity doll category. This was *Patsy*. She was one of the first composition dolls to resemble a real child and was properly proportioned. She was a "modern girl" with bobbed hair and short skirts. She was designed by Bernard Lipfert who also created *Shirley Temple*, the *Dionne Quintuplets, Sonja Henie, Toni®* and many other popular dolls. *Patsy* is credited with being the first American doll to have an extensive ready-made wardrobe and accessories. She is also the first American doll who was joined by a large series of companion dolls.

In 1928, the all-composition *Patsy* had a tempestuous beginning. The December 1927 issue of *Playthings* magazine featured a new Effanbee doll, *Mimi*, who was advertised as the doll who had "IT." "IT" was a description created by popular novelist and screen writer Madame Elinor Glyn to describe the personality of movie flapper Clara Bow. Flappers were modern emancipated women, and this new ideal of beauty was the inspiration for the *Patsy* dolls. In January of 1928, Effanbee displayed the same advertisement only the doll who had "IT" was now called *Patsy*. Effanbee registered the United States trademark "Mi-Mi" (number 256079) and the trademark "Patsy" (number 256080) on October 14, 1927. During 1928, the Effanbee Doll Company was involved in litigation with the Maxine Doll Company of New York City to obtain an injunction against Maxine, whom it claimed was infringing on its design for *Patsy* with a similar doll called *Mitzi*. Maxine, in turn, sued Effanbee and in the Supreme Court of the State of New York on July 30, 1928, won the privilege of producing and selling its similar *Mitzi*. The appellate court later reversed this decision, granting Effanbee exclusive right "to a doll having the features, characteristics and general appearance of *Patsy* as well as the trade name." Effanbee was entitled to receive a trademark registration for *Patsy*, as it had followed the law and had used this name commercially since about 1924.

Books and chapters in doll books have been written about the highly collectible *Patsy* dolls. Of all the doll literature pertaining to the *Patsy* dolls that could be pursued for further study, the author would recommend foremost *The Effanbee Patsy Family & Related Types* by Patricia N. Schoonmaker, Doll Research Projects, 1971. This volume is the most scholarly, precise, detailed and accurate of all those available on the subject.

My purpose here is to illustrate and compare the various types of *Patsy* dolls and to show other collectible dolls from the same time period that were "knockoffs" of this celebrated creation. The outline of the doll's description includes a date which refers to the first issue of the doll. Most *Patsy* dolls were produced and sold until about 1950.

Most of the *Patsy* dolls are fully-jointed composition and have painted features and painted molded hair, tiny closed mouths, and the "bent" right arm, positioned at an angle. Variations of this description are noted throughout the text.

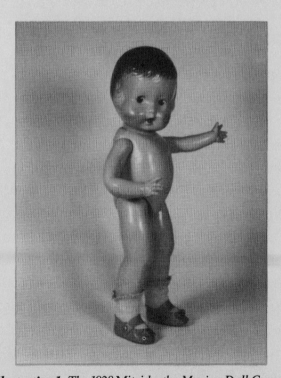

Illustration 1. *The 1928* Mitzi *by the Maxine Doll Company. She is 13¼in (33cm) tall and has brown painted hair and brown painted eyes. The body construction is very close to the design for* Patsy *except that* Mitzi *has a socket head and an open/closed mouth. The shoes and socks are original. She is marked across the back: "'MITZI'//By MAXINE//PAT. PEND."*

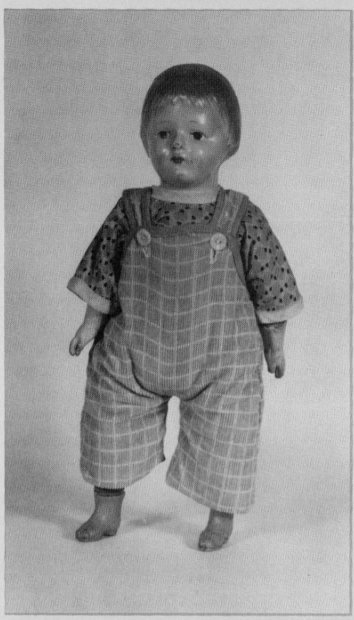

Before the cloth-bodied *Patsy* doll was introduce[d]
by Effanbee in 1924, dolls made of composition compo[ne]nts were becoming more common. Dolls with bisqu[e]
heads were losing popularity because most of them ha[d]
been manufactured in Germany and World War I e[n]ded Germany's dominance in the doll and toy marke[t.]
Composition dolls were also cheaper to make and the[y]
sold for less. Most importantly, they were more durab[le]
than bisque dolls as a casual bump did not shatter the[m]
as it did bisque parts. Composition dolls could b[e]
played with, not just admired. Children were not r[e]stricted to bringing them out only for special occasio[ns]
and handling them with great care, usually under pa[r]ental supervision. The early composition dolls da[te]
from before World War I but until the arrival of the a[ll]
composition *Patsy* they were usually not well-propo[r]tioned in design and construction. The body of the ear[ly]
dolls using composition parts was rather bulky in shap[e]
and was cloth packed tightly with cork bits, rag conten[t,]
cotton batting or other shredded materials. The low[er]
arms and legs were also a composition material bu[t]
generally were too small or too large in relation to th[e]
body size. The heads commanded the most attention i[n]
the modeling and the finishing. Effanbee adopted th[is]
style of doll around 1912 with *Baby Dainty, Bab[y]
Grumpy* and other "unbreakable" dolls.

Illustration 2. *This boy doll of unknown manufactur[e]
would date from the World War I period. The cloth bo[dy]
is stuffed with wood shavings and the arms and legs ar[e]
attached with metal pins. The lower arms and legs an[d]
the head are made of a heavy composition. The hair an[d]
the facial features are painted. The cloth portion of th[e]
legs is brown and white horizontal stripes to represe[nt]
stockings and the composition feet are little molde[d]
boots. The doll, whose head modeling is like what Be[r]nard Lipfert incorporated into his design for* Patsy, *me[a]sures 12½in (32cm) tall.*

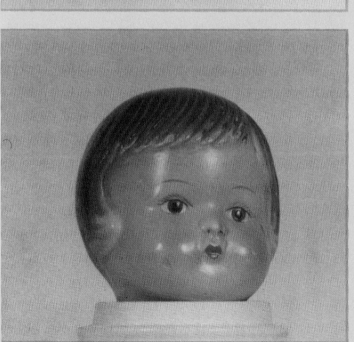

Illustration 3. *The head shown here originally came o[n]
a crude composition body. The molded hair, button nos[e]
and tiny mouth are also reminiscent of the* Patsy-styl[e.]
*The socket head is a heavy papier-mâché and is deft[ly]
painted. The doll probably dates from around the earl[y]
1920s. At the neck the head is marked: "GERMANY//[.]
C 11 1/2."*

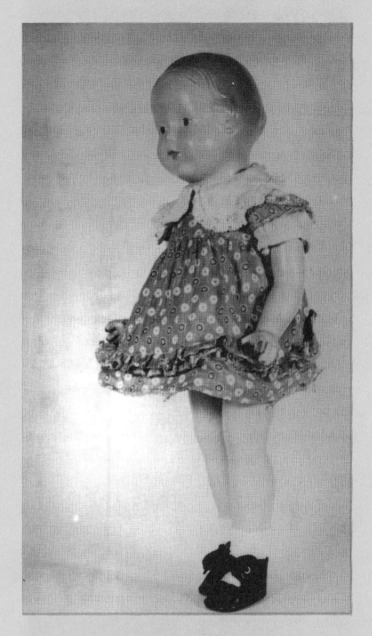

Illustration 4. *16½in (42cm)* Baby Dainty *as a girl doll. The* Baby Dainty *dolls date from around 1912 until well into the 1920s and were made in several different versions. The thickness of the body would determine whether the doll was a baby, a toddler or a girl. This version is too similar to the cloth-bodied* Patsy *seen in Illustration 6 to be coincidental. The full composition legs are from the same mold and even the hair is quite similar. She has reddish hair with a side part, blue painted eyes and a closed mouth. The body is stuffed cloth and the shoulder plate head is marked on the back: "EFFANBEE//DOLLS//WALK.TALK.SLEEP [in an oval]." Variations of this marking were used on different* Effanbee *dolls of the 1920s, such as* Rosemary. *The doll shown here wears a commercial costume of the period but it is not original to her.*

Illustration 5. *Close-up of the 16½in (42cm)* Baby Dainty, *seen in* Illustration 4, *showing the detail of the face and hair modeling.*

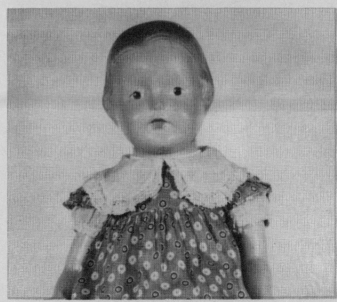

PATSY (cloth body)

Date: After 1924.

Size: 14in (36cm) to 16in (41cm).

Description: Stationary shoulder plate head; full composition arms; full composition legs or lower composition legs only.

Hair: Molded and painted hair or unpainted hair covered with a human hair wig.

Eyes: Blue painted or blue tin sleep eyes.

Mouth: Closed or open with teeth.

Mark: On the back of the shoulder plate:

EFFANBEE PATSY COPYR. DOLL   or   EFFANBEE PATSY

Illustration 6. 15½in (39cm) cloth-bodied Patsy; full legs; painted features; replaced clothing; marked: "EFFANBEE//PATSY//COPR.//DOLL [in a circle]." Rosemary Hanline Collection.

Illustration 7. 14½in (37cm) cloth-bodied Patsy; composition lower legs; tin eyes, open mouth; replaced clothing; marked: "EFFANBEE//PATSY//COPR.// DOLL [in a circle]." Rosemary Hanline Collection.

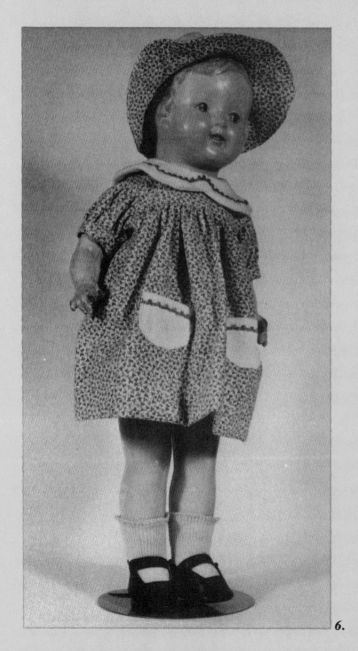

6.

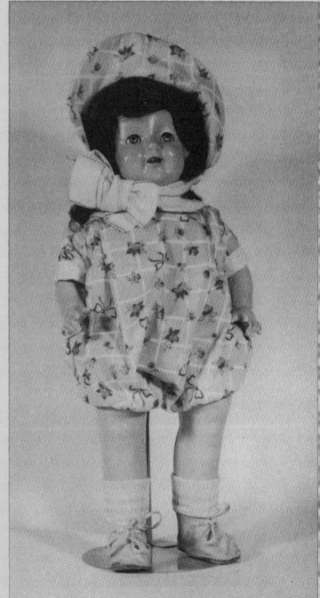

PATSY

Date: 1928.

Size: 13½in (34cm).

Hair: Molded and painted, with or without a molded headband, various shades of red; can also be dark auburn or brown (rarer).

Eyes: Brown painted (blue is much rarer), side-glancing is more common than centered eyes.

Mark: On the shoulders: "EFFanBEE//PATSY//PAT. PEND.//DOLL." (This is the version with the headband and the head is unmarked.) The circa 1933 more common version without the molded headband is marked on the head "EFFanBEE//PATSY" and on the shoulders "EFFanBEE//PATSY//DOLL."

Note: The basic *Patsy* was also dressed as a boy.

Illustration 8. 13½in (34cm) Patsy; auburn hair; brown eyes; all-original in a labeled dress; marked: "EFFanBEE//PATSY//PAT. PEND.//DOLL." Rosemary Hanline Collection.

Illustration 9. 13½in (34cm) Patsy; brown hair; brown eyes; old but not original dress; marked: "EFFanBEE//PATSY//PAT. PEND.//DOLL."

Illustration 10. 13½in (34cm) Patsy; red hair without a headband; light brown eyes; marked on the head "EFFanBEE//PATSY" and on the shoulders "EFFanBEE//PATSY//DOLL."

Illustration 11. 13½in (34cm) Patsy; brown hair; blue eyes; marked on the shoulders: "EFFanBEE//PATSY//PAT. PEND.//DOLL." Rosemary Hanline Collection.

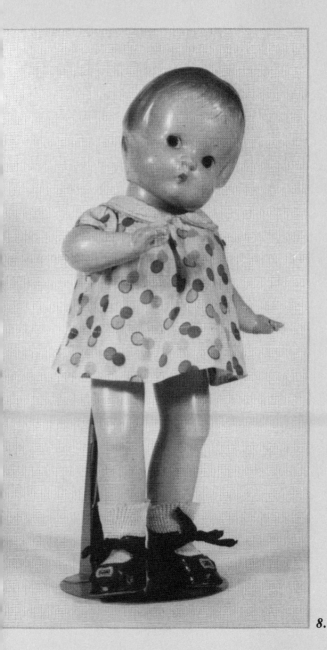

8.

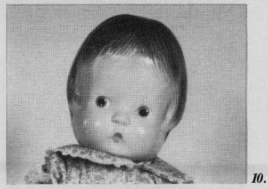

9.

10.

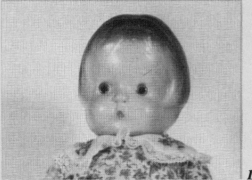

11.

PATSY (sleep eyes)

Hair: Red without headband (circa 1933 mold).
Eyes: Brown or green sleep eyes with eyelashes.
Mark: On the head: "EFFanBEE//PATSY;" on the shoulders: "EFFanBEE//PATSY//DOLL."

Illustration 12. Besides wearing an original Effanbee heart bracelet with her name, this sleep-eyed Patsy is dressed in an all-original cowboy suit. The suede vest, wristbands and chaps are trimmed with nailhead studs and are worn over a red body suit. The shoes are white leatherette with side snaps. The sleep eyes are brown and the hair is a light red. Rosemary Hanline Collection.

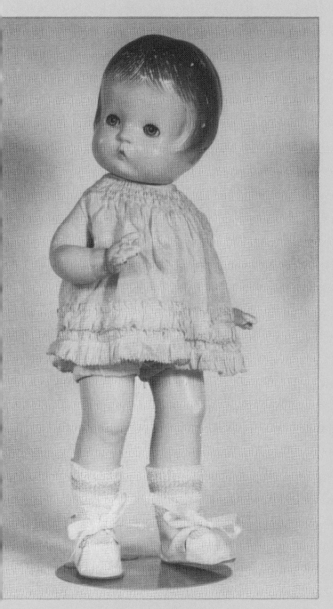

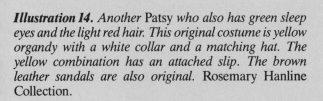

Illustration 14. Another Patsy *who also has green sleep eyes and the light red hair. This original costume is yellow organdy with a white collar and a matching hat. The yellow combination has an attached slip. The brown leather sandals are also original.* Rosemary Hanline Collection.

Illustration 13. Patsy *with light green glass sleep eyes and darker red hair. She is wearing an original dress of light yellow silk with a matching combination undergarment. In general, the green eyes have maintained their clarity better than the brown eyes have. The brown eyes tend to crackle with age. The appearance can be restored with the application of machine oil, but this can cause the composition to soften and it will erase the paint finish, particularly painted eyelashes, if it remains on the surface.*

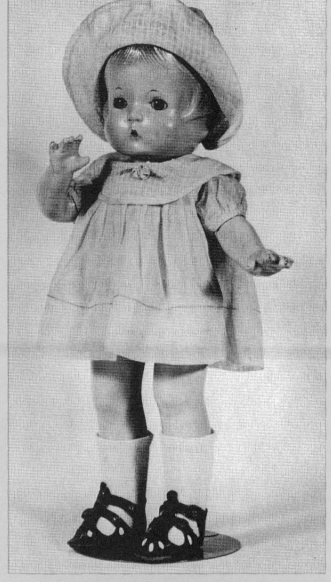

Illustration 15. Patsy Ann *from the book* Patsy Ann Her Happy Times *by Mona Reed King. The book was copyright by Rand McNally in 1935. A similar outfit, worn by* Patsy, *is shown in Illustration 126. It is a red wool two-piece snowsuit with a matching hat. The rubber galoshes also have working zippers.*

Illustration 16. *Some* Patsys *with sleep eyes also have wigs of mohair or human hair in various shades. The doll shown here has a blonde mohair wig and brown sleep eyes. The costume is a replacement fashioned in the* Patsy-*style from the talented hand of Rosemary Hanline. The shoes are also handmade of white leather.* Rosemary Hanline Collection.

Illustration 17. *The most rare of all the* Patsys *is the dark-skinned version. This one has black painted hair and brown painted eyes. She is the earlier version of* Patsy, *incised:* "EFFanBEE//PATSY//PAT. PEND.//DOLL." *The clothing is a copy from the original pattern.* Rosemary Hanline Collection.

16.

Illustration 18. *Advertisement from* Children's Activities *from March 1947, showing the 1946 reissue of* Patsy.

Illustration 19. *The 1946 version of* Patsy *in a copy of the original outfit. This doll is not marked but the molding is almost identical to the earlier* Patsy. *She has red painted hair without a molded headband and blue painted side-glancing eyes with painted eyelashes. This doll is incised "P" on the left hip and "d" on the right leg.*

Illustration 20. *In 1976, the Effanbee Doll Company offered a "limited edition" of a new version of* Patsy *to members of the Effanbee Limited Edition Doll Club. She is a soft fully-jointed vinyl that has a matte luster. She has the traditional molded hair of* Patsy *and blue sleep eyes. She is 16in (41cm) tall and resembles* Patsy Ann *more than* Patsy *although she does not have the "bent" right arm of the standing dolls of the* Patsy *family. She wears a pink organdy dress and her heart bracelet is attached to the left hand with a ribbon.*

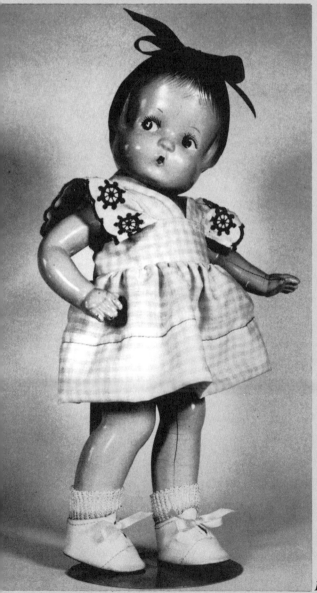

19.

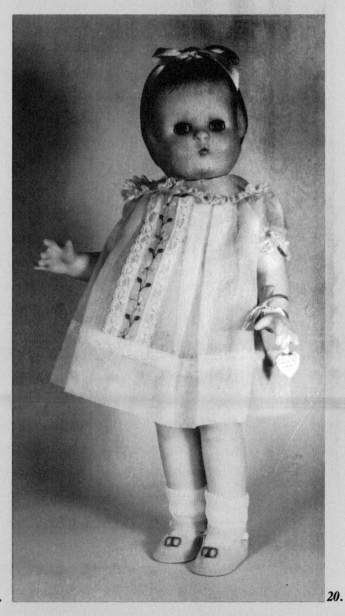

20.

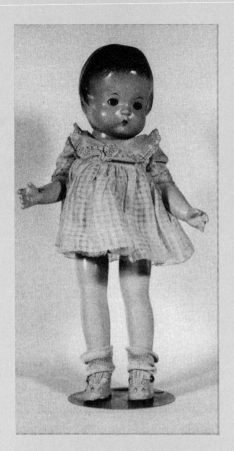

Various combinations of *Patsy* parts were used to form dolls that were original Effanbee factory products. They are considered a part of the *Patsy* family and are more rare than the standard *Patsy* dolls. *Patsy* heads were used on *Patricia* bodies, the early version of *Skippy* had a standard *Patsy* body and *Patsy Baby* heads with curly wigs were "Tousle Head" *Patsys* on *Patsy* bodies, to cite a few of these variations. Others are shown in *Illustrations 44, 45, 61, 74, 75, 83, 84, 92, 93 and 94*. These genuine combinations are not to be confused with dolls that have been constructed from odd parts by collectors.

Illustration 21. 14½in (37cm) Patsy-Patricia *combination. The head has brown molded hair and brown sleep eyes while the body and the limbs are made from the standard* Patricia *mold. The head is marked "EFFanBee//PATSY" and the shoulders are marked "EFFANBEE//PATRICIA." These dolls were marketed under such names as* Little Sister. *This doll wears an original labeled pink cotton dress with a lace-trimmed collar and matching combination underclothing with an attached slip. The T-strap leatherette shoes are pink and so are the stockings.* Rosemary Hanline Collection.

Illustration 22. 12½in (32cm) Skippy *on a* Patsy *body. This is the earlier version of* Skippy *from 1928. He has blonde painted hair with a molded curl dangling down his forehead and blue painted eyes.* Skippy *was advertised as "the Boy Friend of Patsy." He originated as a cartoon character in the 1920s by P. L. Crosby and became even more famous in the 1931 film in which Jackie Cooper played Skippy. This doll wears a copy of the original outfit of a matching navy blue coat, hat and short pants and also a white shirt, red necktie and red and white striped stockings. The original pin from Effanbee says that* Skippy *is "The Real American Boy."* Rosemary Hanline Collection.

Other *Skippy* dolls from the 1930s have cloth bodies with full composition legs or swing legs that have molded and painted shoes and stockings and measure 14½in (37cm). During World War II, *Skippy* dolls were dressed in the uniforms of the American servicemen, with painted shoes and stockings. *Skippys* are marked on the head: "EFFANBEE//SKIPPY//©//P.L. Crosby [in script]." *Skippys* with *Patsy* bodies are marked across the shoulders: "EFFanBEE//PATSY//PAT. PEND.// DOLL."

Illustration 23. Jackie Cooper and Mitzi Green in the movie Skippy.

WEE PATSY

Date: 1934.
Size: 5¾in (15cm).
Description: All-composition with movable arms and legs only.
Hair: Molded and painted red with a headband.
Eyes: Blue painted, side-glancing or straight forward.
Mark: Across the shoulders: "EFFANBEE//WEE PATSY."

The *Wee Patsy* doll, one of the more difficult to find of the *Patsy* series, was a dolls' house doll and was used as an advertising promotion for the Colleen Moore dolls' house that was placed on exhibition around the country during 1935. Colleen Moore, born in 1900, was the movie star who invented the flapper image for the 1923 film *Flaming Youth*.

Illustration 24. *5¾in (15cm) all-original* Wee Patsy *in a red and white cotton dress. The Colleen Moore pin is yellow on a red background.* Patricia Gardner Collection.

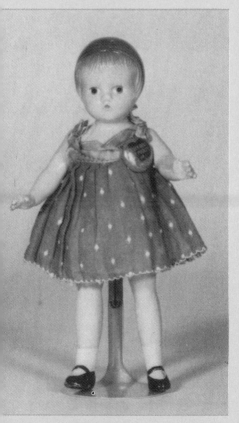

Illustration 25. *5¾in (15cm) all-original* Wee Patsy *in a dark blue organdy dress. Her pin has a gold background with a red heart. These dolls were the "Fairy Princess" from the "castle," but there was no dolls' house for them, although the original box shows a picture of a dolls' house. A boy version was also available.* Marge Meisinger Collection.

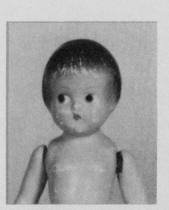

Illustration 27. Colleen Moore from Flaming Youth.

Illustration 26. *5¾in (15cm)* Wee Patsy *with the unusual side-glancing eyes.*

PATSY (BABY) TINYETTE

Date: 1933.
Size: Baby, 6½in (17cm); toddler, 7¾in (20cm).
Description: Baby with curved arms and legs; toddler with curved arms and straight legs.
Hair: Yellow, red or brown painted (brown is the most common).
Eyes: Brown or blue painted.
Mark: On the head: "EFFANBEE;" on the shoulders: "EFFANBEE//BABY TINYETTE."

Note: The straight-leg toddler is more rare than the bent-limb baby version. The dolls are marked "Baby Tinyette" but were advertised as *Patsy Tinyette*.

Illustration 28. *6½in (17cm) all-original baby version of Tinyette. She has red hair and brown eyes. She is sitting in her original wicker trunk that includes a cotton covered mattress, additional clothing and a nursing bottle.*

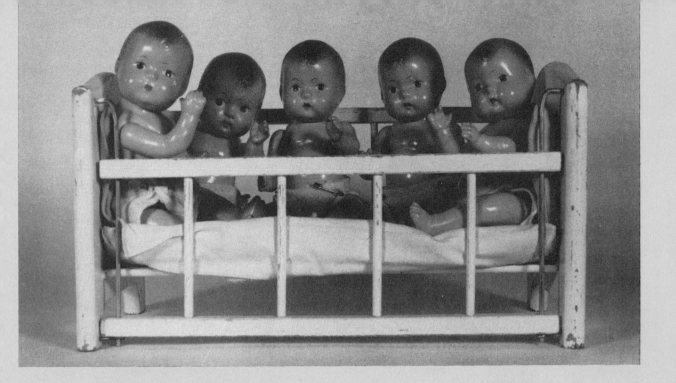

Illustration 29. *Quintuplet* Tinyettes *that were sold in competition with Madame Alexander's* Dionne Quintuplets, *although they could not be advertised as such. These Quints have brown painted hair and blue eyes, although other sets have brown eyes, more in keeping with the Dionnes. They wear their original diapers and are posing in a bed that belongs to Vogue's* Ginnette.

Illustration 30. *7³⁄₄in (20cm)* Tinyette *toddlers in original labeled outfits. Both have brown hair and blue eyes. The boy has brown pants and a plaid shirt while the girl wears a pink organdy outfit with matching shoes.*

Illustration 31. *7³⁄₄in (20cm) all-original* Tinyette *in a green-dotted white organdy outfit. She has brown hair and blue eyes.* Rosemary Hanline Collection.

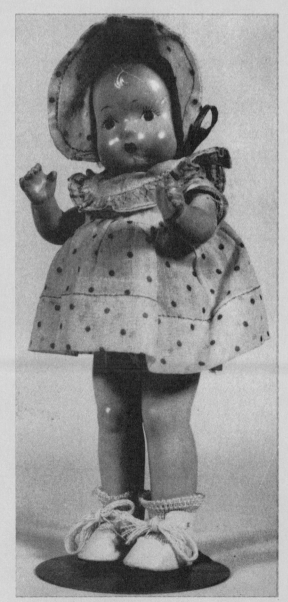

32.

PATSYETTE

Date: 1931.
Size: 9½in (24cm).
Hair: Red painted.
Eyes: Brown and blue painted (blue is more rare).
Mark: On the shoulders: "EFFANBEE//PATSYETTE//DOLL."

Note: There are also dark-skinned versions of *Patsyette* with black hair.

Illustration 32. *The rare blue-eyed version of a 9½in (24cm) Pat-syette. Rosemary Hanline Collection.*

Illustration 33. *9½in (24cm) all-original* Patsyette *in a cotton print dress wearing the original gold paper tag.*

Illustration 34. *9½in (24cm)* Patsyette *twins dressed as a girl and a boy. They wear all-original red and white cotton outfits with matching hats.*

33.

Patsyette also came with mohair wigs of various colors. The wig is set into a hole that is drilled into the center of the top of the head and is glued over unpainted molded hair. Wigged versions of *Patsyette* are less common than those with painted hair.

Illustration 35. 9¹/₂in (24cm) blue-eyed *Patsyette with an auburn mohair wig in bangs and braids. Rosemary Hanline Collection.*

Illustration 36. 9¹/₂in (24cm) all-original "Little Red Riding Hood" *version of* Patsyette. *She has an auburn wig and brown eyes.* Rosemary Hanline Collection.

Illustration 37. 9¹/₂in (24cm) *brown-eyed version of* Patsyette *with a blonde mohair wig. She wears an original dress of pale green organdy with a matching bonnet trimmed in a contrasting shade. The white shoes are also original.*

35.

36.

37.

PATSY BABYETTE

Date: Circa 1930.
Size: 9in (23cm).
Description: Baby with curved arms and legs.
Hair: Yellow, red or brown painted (yellow is the
    most rare), caracul wigs over unpainted
    hair.
Eyes: Blue or brown glass sleep eyes (brown tin
    sleep eyes are rare).
Mark: On the head: "EFFANBEE;" on the
    shoulders: "EFFANBEE//PATSY BA-
    BYETTE."

Illustration 38. *This 9in (23cm)* Patsy Babyette *is rather rare becau[se] she has yellow painted hair and brown tin sleep eyes. The pi[nk] organdy dress and matching bonnet are original.*

Illustration 39. *9in (23cm)* Patsy Babyette *boy and girl twins [in] original outfits of blue and white, with reddish-brown hair and bl[ue] sleep eyes. Rosemary Hanline Collection.*

Illustration 40. *9in (23cm)* Patsy Babyette *with a light brown carac[ul] fur wig and blue sleep eyes. Rosemary Hanline Collection.*

38.

39.

4[0.]

41.

PATSY BABY

Date: 1932.
Size: 10in (25cm) to 11in (28cm) (all-composition versions).
Description: Curved arms and legs (variations are shown in *Illustrations 44* and *45*).
Hair: Yellow, light brown or dark brown painted (the earlier versions have the yellow hair).
Eyes: Green, blue or brown sleep eyes.
Mark: On the head: "EFFanBee//PATSY BABY;" on the body: "Effanbee//'PATSY BABY'."

Note: The dolls are marked "Patsy Baby," but they were advertised as *Patsy Babykin*.

Illustration 41. 10in (25cm) Patsy Baby *with yellow painted hair and green sleep eyes.*

Illustration 42. 11in (28cm) Patsy Babykin *with light brown hair and blue sleep eyes. She is all-original with a dotted swiss outfit. This is one of the later versions of the* Patsy Babykin, *which was manufactured until the late 1940s.*

Illustration 43. The original box for the 11in (28cm) Patsy Babykin, *seen in* Illustration 42.

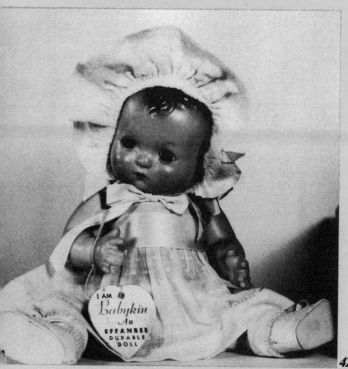

42.

43.

The Patsy Baby came in several variations. Among them is a black baby that had either sleep or painted eyes with three inset yarn tufts of hair. Another of the more rare combinations was created by shortages of supplies during World War II. This edition has the standard head set into a pink muslin body with a wooden neck plug and also has composition hands. The cloth-bodied baby has blue sleep eyes and darker brown painted hair. A different variation is the *Patsy* "Baby Toddler" or the "Tousle Head" *Patsy*. It is a *Patsy Baby* head with a curly caracul wig on the standard *Patsy* body. These versions are harder to find.

Illustration 44. *13in (33cm)* Patsy Baby *with the cloth body; brown hair and blue sleep eyes; marked on the head: "EFFANBEE//PATSY BABY."* Rosemary Hanline Collection.

Illustration 45. Patsy *"Baby Toddler"* or *"Tousle He..* Patsy; *marked "EFFANBEE//PATSY BABY" on head and "EFFANBEE//PATSY//DOLL" on the b... This is a factory combination and not a put-together. ... has a caracul wig and green sleep eyes. The clothing ... the shoes are handmade replacements.* Rosemary H...ine Collection.

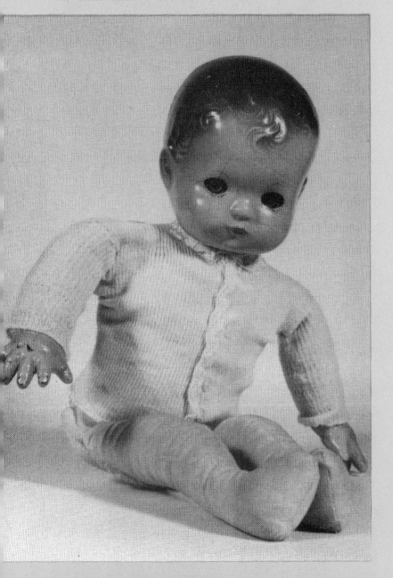

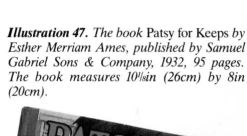

Illustration 47. *The book* Patsy for Keeps *by Esther Merriam Ames, published by Samuel Gabriel Sons & Company, 1932, 95 pages. The book measures 10¹/₈in (26cm) by 8in (20cm).*

stration 46. Close-up of an all-original Patsy, *seen in* Illustration 14. *emary Hanline Collection.*

Illustration 48. *The book* Patsy Ann Her Happy Times *by Mona Reed King, published by Rand McNally & Company, 1935, 64 pages, 5¹/₂in (14cm) by 6⁵/₈in (17cm).*

lustration 49. Colleen Moore's Doll House Cut-*uts, copyrighted by the Ullman Mfg. Co., 1934, 14 ges of heavy stock paper. The real miniature castle uilt for Colleen Moore cost her $100,000 and mea-red 9 feet square and 14 feet high and was scaled 1in cm) equals 1ft (31cm). The dolls' house toured Amer-a under Miss Moore's personal supervision and the roceeds from the exhibition were given to charities ring for the crippled children in each city. The* Wee *tsy dolls tied into this publicity, even though they did t actually represent a "fairy princess" or a "fairy ince." The book measures 10in (25cm) by 14¹/₄in 6cm).*

PATSY JR.

Date: 1930.
Size: 11½in (29cm).
Hair: Red painted with a molded headband (a rarer version has brown painted hair).
Eyes: Brown or blue painted (blue is rarer).
Mark: On the shoulders: "EFFANBEE// PATSY JR.//DOLL."

Note: *Patsy Jr.* was advertised as *Patsykins.* Variations are shown in *Illustrations 52* through *55.*

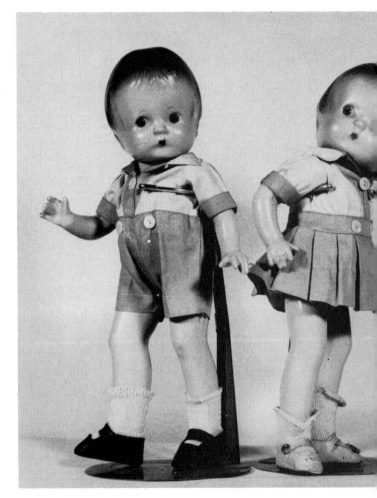

Illustration 50. *11½in (29cm)* Patsy Jr. *with red hair and brown eyes. She is all-original and wears a red wool skirt with an attached white cotton blouse, a red and white knit pullover sweater with a matching scarf, stockings trimmed in red and red shoes.*

Illustration 51. *11½in (29cm)* Patsy Jr. *twins in all-original outfits of green and white. They both have red hair and brown eyes. Rosemary Hanline Collection.*

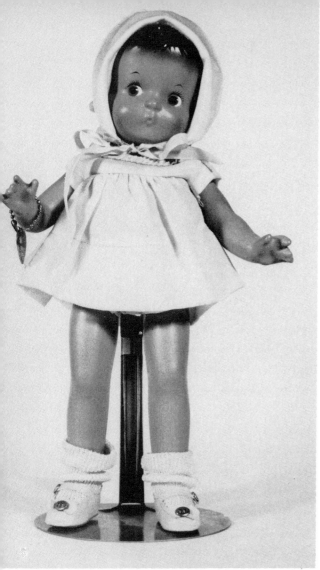

52.

53.

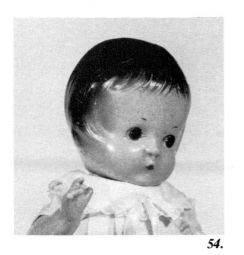

54.

55.

Illustration 52. 11½in (29cm) rare dark-skinned Patsy Jr. with black hair and brown eyes. She wears an all-original pink crepe labeled dress, bonnet and combination undies. The snap shoes are also pink. Rosemary Hanline Collection.
Illustration 53. 11½in (29cm) rare Patsy Jr. in an all-original Dutch costume. She has a blonde mohair wig over unpainted molded hair and blue sleep eyes. She carries her original paper tag as well as her Effanbee heart bracelet and is in like-new condition. Rosemary Hanline Collection. *Illustration 54.* 11½in (29cm) rare Patsy Jr. with the unusual brown molded hair and blue painted eyes. Rosemary Hanline Collection. *Illustration 55.* 11½in (29cm) rare Patsy Jr. with an unusual combination of brown molded hair and blue sleep eyes. Rosemary Hanline Collection.

Illustration 56. *Close-up of* Patricia Kin *with a* Patsy Jr. *body.*

Illustration 57. Patsy, *marked on the shoulders:* "EFFanBEE//PATSY//PAT. PEND.//DOLL."

Illustration 58. *The* Patsy *family, from left to right:* Patsy Lou, Patsy Ann, Patsy Joan, Patsy *(from 1946)*, Patsy Jr., Patsyette *and* Tinyette *"Toddler."*

Illustration 59. *Close-up of a* Skippy *with a* Patsy *body.*

Illustration 62. *Close-up of a* Baby Tinyette.

ation 60. *Close-up of a* Patsyette
lue eyes.

Illustration 61. *"Tousle Head"* Mary Lee *with a* Patsy Joan *body.*

Illustration 63. Patricia.

Illustration 64. 11½in (29cm) Patricia Kin, *another rare factory combination from Effanbee, with a dark blonde human hair wig, blue sleep eyes and a closed mouth. The green cotton dress with attached panties is original. The head is marked: "EFFANBEE//PATRICIA KIN." The body of the doll is the standard* Patsy Jr. *mold and is marked as such.* Rosemary Hanline Collection.

PATSY JOAN

Date: 1932.
Size: 16in (41cm).
Hair: Red molded and painted or unpainted molded hair covered with a wig of human hair or mohair of various shades.
Eyes: Brown, green or blue sleep eyes.
Mark: On shoulders: "EFFanBEE//'PATSY-JOAN'."

Illustration 65. *16in (41cm)* Patsy Joan *with a bright red mohair wig and green sleep eyes. Rosemary Hanline Collection.*

Illustration 66. *16in (41cm)* Patsy Joan *with an auburn human hair wig, brown sleep eyes and painted fingernails.*

Illustration 67. *16in (41cm)* Patsy Joan *with the typical red painted hair and green glass eyes, wearing her all-original outfit of blue organdy with matching hat.*

65.

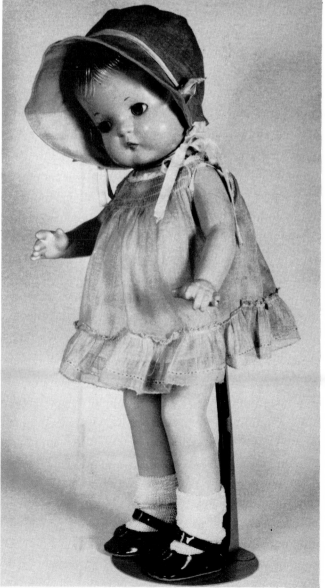

66.

67.

Illustration 68. *Close-up of the 16in (41cm) un-marked Patsy-type seen in* Illustration 108, *with red painted hair and blue eyes.*

Illustration 69. *Close-up of the 15in (38cm) unmarked Patsy-type, seen in* Illustration 105, *with brown deeply molded painted hair and blue painted eyes with heavy eyelashes and eye shadow.*

Illustration 70. 8½in (22cm) Babykin *purchased new in 1975 for $7.00. She is fully-jointed and made of vinyl with painted hair, blue sleep eyes and is an open-mouthed nurser. She sits next to her original box and is wearing a pink flannel hooded jacket and bunting blanket. Her head is marked:* "EFFANBEE."

Illustration 71. 6¼in (16cm) painted bisque girl of the typical Patsy modeling. *She has jointed arms and legs, black painted hair with a hairband, dark painted eyes and painted shoes and stockings like* Wee Patsy. *Her dress is a replacement. She is marked on the back:* "MADE IN//JAPAN//S/092."

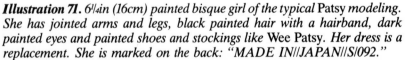

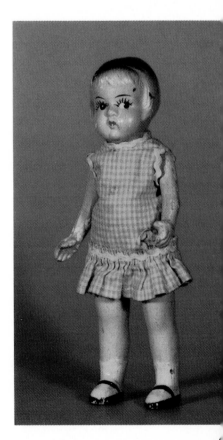

70.

Patricia and *Mary Lee* are part of the *Patsy* family of dolls. They were advertised as "the grown-up sisters of the famous Patsy Doll Family."

PATRICIA

Date: 1932.
Size: 14½in (37cm).
Description: All-composition with both arms slightly curved.
Hair: Plain head covered with a mohair or human hair wig in various shades.
Eyes: Brown, green or blue sleep eyes.
Mouth: Closed.
Mark: On the shoulders: "EFFANBEE//'PATRICIA'."

Illustration 72. 14½in (37cm) Patricia, *with a Patricia body, a light brown human hair wig and brown sleep eyes. She wears an original cotton dress with a matching combination undergarment.* Rosemary Hanline Collection.

Illustration 73. 14½in (37cm) Patricia, *with a Patricia body, a blonde human hair wig and green sleep eyes.* Rosemary Hanline Collection.

MARY LEE

Date: 1932.
Size: 16½in (42cm).
Description: Composition head, arms (slightly curved) and legs on a cloth body or fully-jointed composition using the *Patsy Joan* body.
Hair: Plain head with wig.
Eyes: Blue, green or brown sleep eyes.
Mouth: Open with four upper teeth and a felt tongue.
Mark: On the head: "©//MARY-LEE."

Illustration 74. 16½in (42cm) Mary Lee, *with a Patsy Joan body, a light brown human hair wig and light brown sleep eyes.* Rosemary Hanline Collection.

Illustration 75. 16½in (42cm) *"Tousle Head"* Mary Lee, *with a Patsy Joan body, a brown caracul wig and brown sleep eyes. She is wearing her original brown plaid cotton jumper over a blouse with attached matching bloomers.* Rosemary Hanline Collection.

73.

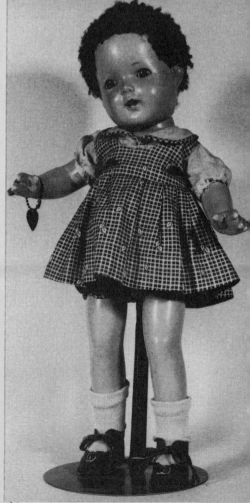

72.   74. 75.

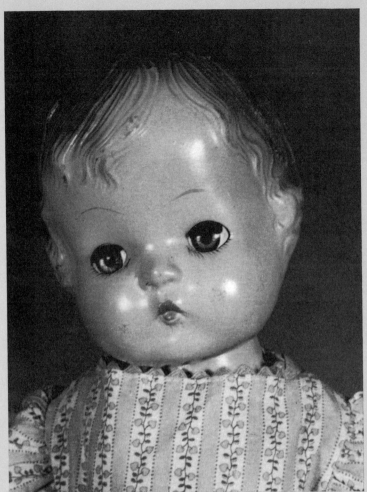

PATSY JOAN (1946)

Date: 1946.
Size: 17in (43cm).
Description: Both arms slightly curved.
Hair: Brown molded and painted.
Eyes: Sleep eyes (probably blue only).
Mark: Across the shoulders: "EFFANDBEE."

Note: This is a comparatively rare doll.

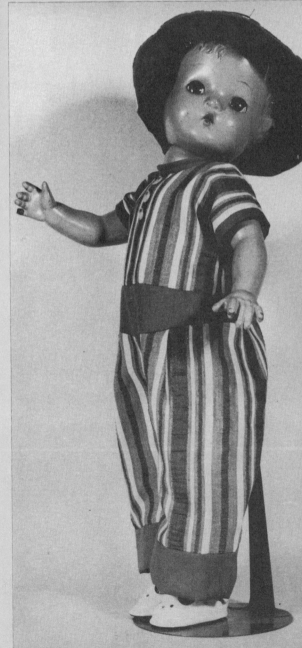

Illustration 76. Close-up of a 17in (43cm) Patsy Joan, showing the detail of the modeling of the face.

Illustration 77. 17in (43cm) Patsy Joan *shown wearing replacement clothing that would be typical of the original* Patsy Joan *era. She was dressed by the Effanbee factory in contemporary little girl costumes of the late 1940s, like dresses and pinafores of cotton with matching bonnets.*

PATSY ANN

Date: 1928.

Size: 19in (48cm).

Hair: Red molded and painted or unpainted and covered with a human hair or mohair wig of various shades.

Eyes: Blue, brown or green tin or glass sleep eyes (some of the tin eyes are also a gray-blue color).

Mark: Across the shoulders: "EFFANBEE//'PATSY-ANN'//©// PAT.# 1283558."

Illustration 78. 19in (48cm) Patsy Ann *with reddish-brown painted hair and gray tin sleep eyes. The yellow cotton beach pajamas and matching hat are from the 1930s and carry a label that reads: "NIKO// FITS PATSY ANN."*

Illustration 79. *Close-up of the 19in (48cm)* Patsy Ann, *seen in* Illustration 78, *showing the detail of the modeling of the face.*

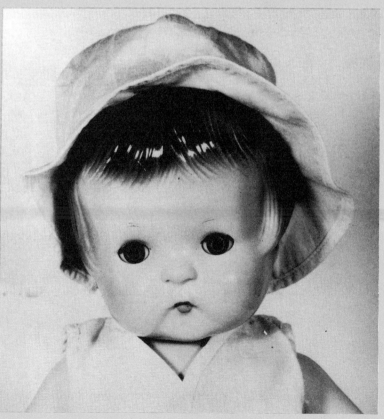

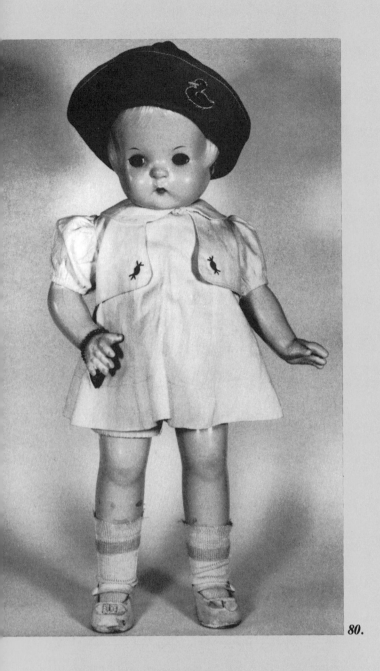

80.

81.

82.

Illustration 80. *19in (48cm)* Patsy Ann *with brown glass sleep eyes. She originally wore a wig over the unpainted molded hair. The heavy cotton dress of pale yellow with attached underpants is original, as are the shoes and stockings.* Patsy Joan *was also presented wearing this identical outfit.*

Illustration 81. *Close-up of a 19in (48cm)* Patsy Ann *with a long red human hair wig and perfect green glass eyes. Rosemary Hanline Collection.*

Illustration 82. *Close-up of a 19in (48cm)* Patsy Ann *with a blonde human hair wig and brown glass eyes. Rosemary Hanline Collection.*

The open-mouthed *Patsy Ann* and the "Tousle Head" *Patsy Ann* used the *Lovums* head with a typical Patsy Ann body. They are Effanbee factory products, not put-together dolls. The *Lovums* doll was a cloth-bodied baby from the same time period as *Patsy Ann* and was marked as such on the attached shoulder plate. These versions of *Patsy Ann* are more rare than those with the typical head.

Illustration 83. *19in (48cm) open-mouthed* Patsy Ann *with a long brown human hair wig, brown eyes and a deep dimple in her chin. This is the* Lovums *head with a smiling mouth with six upper teeth and a tongue. The clothing is replaced.* Rosemary Hanline Collection.

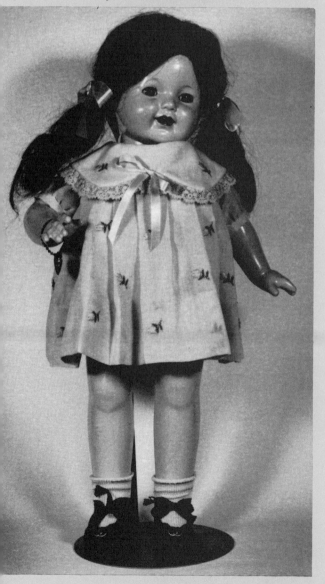

Illustration 84. *19in (48cm) "Tousle Head"* Patsy Ann, *also with the* Lovums *head. The head is the same as on the* Patsy Ann *seen in* Illustration 83. *This one has a blonde caracul wig that has lost its curls and brown sleep eyes. The dress is replaced but the side snap shoes and the stockings are original.* Rosemary Hanline Collection.

Illustration 85. Patsy Ann *from the book* Patsy Ann Her Happy Times *by Mona Reed King.*

Illustration 86. *This vinyl doll from 1959 was called* Patsy Ann, *although she bears only a slight resemblance to the original* Patsy *dolls. There was also a vinyl doll called* Patsy. *Her soft vinyl head has rooted blonde hair, blue sleep eyes and freckles sprinkled across the bridge of her nose. She is 15in (38cm) tall and dressed in her original costume. Her head is marked: "EFFANBEE//PATSY ANN//© 1959." Her fully-jointed body is rigid vinyl and is marked across the shoulders: "E F F A N B E E." Her shoes are also made of vinyl.* Rosemary Hanline Collection.

Illustration 87. *15in (38cm) vinyl* Patsy Ann, *from 1959, with a soft vinyl head which has rooted blonde hair, blue sleep eyes and freckles sprinkled across the bridge of the nose. Her costume is original and she is marked on the head: "EFFANBEE//PATSY ANN//© 1959." Her rigid vinyl body is fully-jointed and she is marked across the shoulders: "E F F A N B E E."*

85.

86.

PATSY LOU

Date: Circa 1930.
Size: 22in (56cm).
Hair: Red molded and painted or unpainted and covered with a
mohair or human hair wig of various shades.
Eyes: Green, blue and brown sleep eyes.
Mark: On the shoulders: "EFFanBEE//'PATSY LOU'."

Illustration 88. *22in (56cm)* Patsy Lou *with brown sleep eyes and replaced clothing.* Rosemary Hanline Collection.

Illustration 89. *22in (56cm)* Patsy Lou *with red painted hair and perfect green sleep eyes. The dress is a copy of the original and utilizes the original collar of yellow chiffon.* Rosemary Hanline Collection.

88.

89.

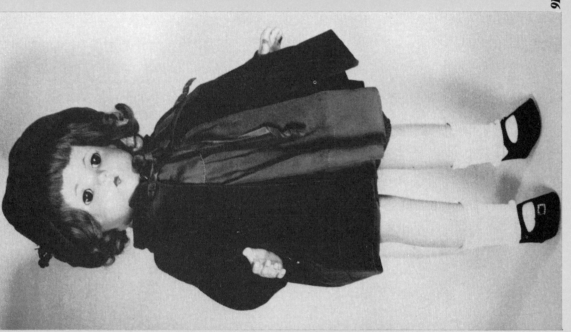

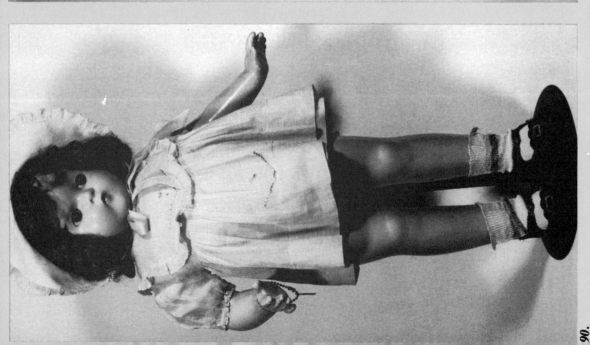

Illustration 90. 22in (56cm) Patsy Lou with an auburn mohair wig and brown sleep eyes. *The clothing is all-original and labeled. The sheer blue cotton dress has embroidery trim and the bonnet and the slip with attached underpants match. The black leatherette shoes have center snaps. Rosemary Hanline Collection. Illustration 91.* 22in (56cm) Patsy Lou with a blonde human hair wig over the unpainted molded hair and brown sleep eyes. *She wears an all-original costume that is a sheer red silk dress with matching undergarments and a red velvet coat and hat. The shoes are black leatherette. Illustration 92.* This 23½in (60cm) Patsy Lou variant has a light brown human hair wig over unpainted molded hair and brown sleep eyes. *Her arms are also the standard Patsy Lou arms but the torso and the legs are longer and slimmer. The component parts all match and the doll appears to be an Effanbee factory product. The*

PATSY RUTH

Date: Circa mid 1930s.

Size: 25in (64cm) to 27in (69cm).

Description: All-composition and fully-jointed in the 27in (69cm) size while the 25in (64cm) size has a composition head, arms and legs on a cloth body with a shoulder plate marked: "EFFANBEE//LOVUMS//©//PAT NO 1283558." Both arms are slightly curved and only the lower parts of the legs are composition.

Hair: Wig, usually of human hair, of various shades over a plain head.

Eyes: Green or brown sleep eyes.

Mark: On the head: "EFFANBEE//PATSY RUTH."

Illustration 93. 25in (64cm) Patsy Ruth *on the* Lovums *shoulder plate with a cloth body. She has a long blonde human hair wig and perfect green sleep eyes. Rosemary Hanline Collection.*

PATSY MAE

Date: Circa mid 1930s.

Size: 28in (71cm) to 30in (76cm).

Description: Composition head, arms and legs on a cloth body with the *Lovums* shoulder plate. Both arms are slightly curved and only the lower parts of the legs are composition.

Hair: Wig, usually of human hair, of various shades over a plain head.

Eyes: Green or brown sleep eyes.

Mark: On the head: "EFFANBEE//PATSY-MAE."

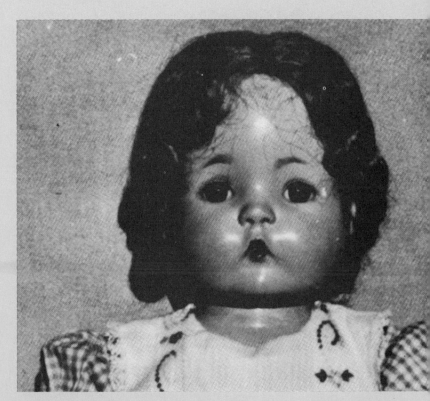

Illustration 94. 30in (76cm) Patsy Mae *with the* Lovums *shoulder plate on a cloth body. She has a blonde human hair wig in the original curls and brown glass eyes. Patricia N. Schoonmaker Collection. Photograph by John Schoonmaker.*

During the 1930s and the 1940s, the leading doll manufacturers, Effanbee included, produced popular play dolls which incorporated the features and the styling of the *Patsy* dolls. There were also countless unmarked and unknown dolls of this type advertised during the period. Most of the unmarked dolls were sold through catalog distribution sources like Montgomery Ward and Sears, Roebuck and Co. or by five-and-ten-cent stores like Woolworth's and G. C. Murphy. Almost all composition doll parts were molded and cast by companies which specialized in this process and then distributed them to the respective doll company or dealer who finished and dressed the dolls. The "marked" dolls from the leading companies (who controlled their own molds) were usually quality products. The unmarked and unknown dolls were of varying degrees of quality with regard to finished and costuming.

Illustration 95. On the left is a 9in (23cm) all-composition fully-jointed girl with brown molded painted hair and blue side-glancing eyes. She dates from the late 1920s and the body construction is similar to that of Patsyette, although the torso is slimmer. The clothing she is wearing is replaced. The doll is marked on the back "EFFANBEE//MADE IN U.S.A."

On the right is an 8in (20cm) toddler similar to the Patsy Tinyette *toddler*. She is Button Nose from the late 1930s and has brown painted hair and blue raised side-glancing eyes. Her cotton print dress with matching underpants may be original. She is marked on the back "EFFANBEE."

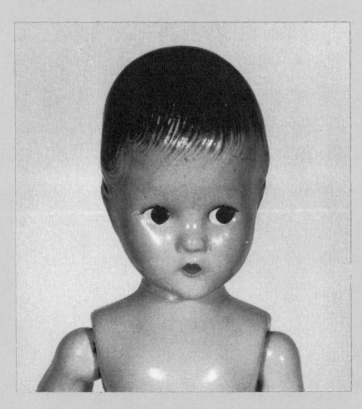

Illustration 96. 11⅛in (28cm) all-composition fully-jointed Suzette, from 1939, with brown molded painted hair and painted blue eyes. Another version of this doll has a plain head covered with a wig. She is marked on the head: "SUZETTE//EFFANBEE//USA;" and on the back "SUZETTE//EFFANBEE//MADE IN//USA.

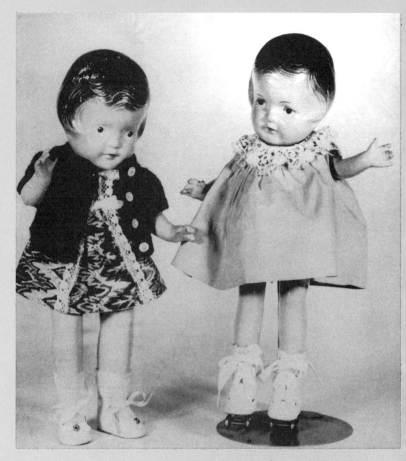

Illustration 97. *12in (31cm) all-composition fully-jointed* **Nancy** *by Arranbee, circa 1930s, with reddish molded painted hair and blue painted eyes. She wears an original pale green cotton dress with a matching hat and matching one-piece undergarment. The dress label reads:* "NANCY//AN ARRANBEE DOLL." *Arranbee's* **Nancy** *also came in other sizes and styles. The doll is marked on the back:* "ARRANBEE//DOLL Co."

Illustration 98. *12in (31cm)* Nancys *by Arranbee. The* **Nancy** *on the left has brown painted hair, blue painted eyes and is marked like the* Nancy *shown in* Illustration 97. *The* **Nancy** *on the right has light red painted hair and blue eyes. She is marked on the back:* "NANCY." *These* Nancys *all have a "bent" right arms like* Patsy *and her family.*

Illustration 99. *8½in (22cm) fully-jointed Dutch twins by Arranbee standing in front of their original suitcase box. They have yellow painted hair with yellow yarn hair attached to their hats. They have blue painted eyes and are reminiscent of* Patsyette. *Their all-original costumes are cotton and flannel and they wear carved wooden shoes that are nailed to their feet. The dolls are marked on the back:* "R & B//DOLL CO."

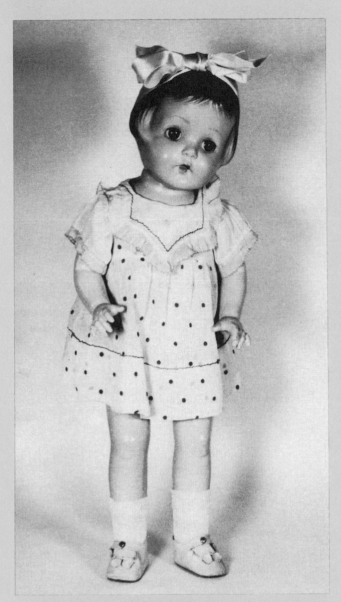

Illustration 100. 27½in (70cm) Sally *by American Character, circa 1930s, with a composition head on a shoulder plate and composition arms and legs attached to a cloth body; red molded painted hair in the* Patsy-*style; brown sleep eyes with eyelashes. Her outfit is all-original and she is marked on the head: "PETITE//SALLY."*

Illustration 101. 13in (33cm) all-composition fully-jointed Betty *by Madame Alexander, 1935, with the "bent" right arm like* Patsy; *blonde mohair wig over molded unpainted hair; blue tin sleep eyes with eyelashes. The doll is not marked but her dress label reads:*

BETTY
MADAME ALEXANDER
NEW YORK

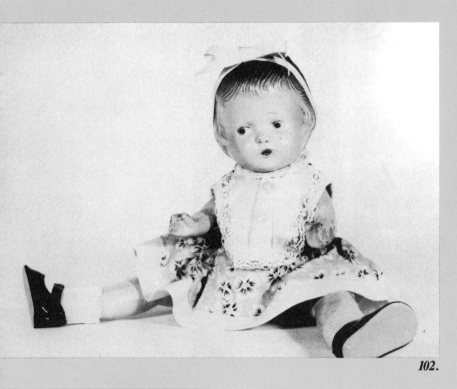

102.

Sensational value

12-inch composition doll $1.08
with doll trunk and com-
plete outfit.   A dream of a dolly
dressed like you might want to be
...She wears a cotton poplin
basque style dress trimmed with
rick-rack and she also has a printed
cotton coat, a blue cotton flannel
cape, matching beret, two pairs of
shoes, socks and snap lock handled
trunk. Shipping weight, 1 pound.
49 P 3548.................$1.08

103.

The all-composition dolls with painted hair and painted eyes were advertised in the wholesale and retail catalogs during the 1930s and the 1940s. Some of them were very similar to the *Patsy* dolls while others deliberately copied the name. These dolls are not marked.

Illustration 102. The 1942 Sears, Roebuck and Co. Christmas catalog advertised a doll, seen in Illustration 103, *that seems to be the one shown here. The body seams are poorly sanded and not much care was taken in the painting of her features and blue eyes so that she could be sold at an economical price.*

Illustration 103. Original advertisement from the 1942 Sears, Roebuck and Co. Christmas catalog for a doll which appears to be like the one shown in Illustration 102.

Illustration 104. This 12in (31cm) all-composition girl has hair that is almost like that of Patsy except that it is painted a light brown color. The eyes are painted blue. Both arms are slightly "bent." The John Plain Catalog for 1938 shows a doll that appears to be this one. She was called Patsy Ann with a "naturally shaped composition body, movable arms and legs." In the same way that Effanbee advertised the Patsys, this doll would "stand alone when you tell her to!"

104.

Illustration 105. *15in (38cm) all-composition fully-jointed girl who seems to be the identical doll shown in the advertisement from the 1943 Sears, Roebuck and Co. Christmas catalog, seen in* Illustration 106. *She has brown very deeply molded painted hair and blue painted eyes with heavy eyelashes and eye shadow. She is another economically produced product and her torso is identical to that of the* Patsy *mold, although the arms and legs are thinner. She is all-original in a matching print dress and bonnet. The white shoes are oilcloth.*
She can be seen close-up in Illustration 69.

Illustration 106. *Original advertisement from the 1943 Sears, Roebuck and Co. Christmas catalog for a doll which appears to be identical to the one seen in* Illustration 105.

Illustration 108. *16in (41cm)* Patsy *variant with red painted red hair and blue eyes. She is all-original and wears a pink slip and underwear with white oilcloth shoes. She can be seen close-up in* Illustration 68.

105.

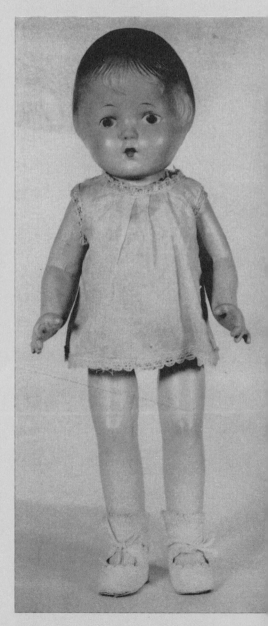

E • 15-in. Standing Doll. . . $1.17

106.

Illustration 107. *The hair modeling on this 14in (36cm)* Patsy-type *is curlier and brown and she has blue painted eyes. She has full composition legs that are of the same mold as those of* Patsy, *but the arms are from the same mold as the two dolls seen in* Illustration 109 *and again are small in relation to the body size. The head is stationary on a shoulder plate and the body is cloth stuffed with excelsior.*

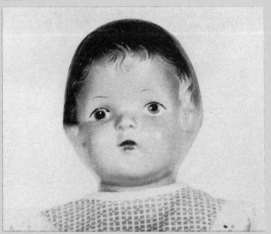

107.

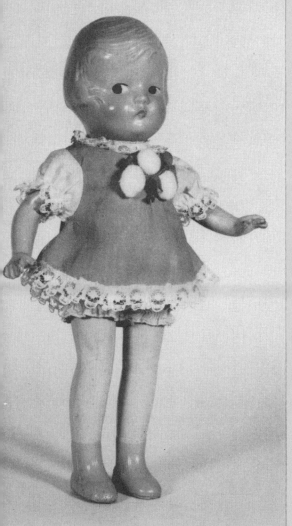

Illustration 109. *These 12in (31cm) twins are very similar to* Patsy Jr. *with painted hair and brown painted eyes. Both arms are in the "bent" position. The doll on the left is wearing her original yellow organdy dress, combination undergarment, shoes and stockings. The twin at the right is modeling the simply designed organdy combination undergarment. They look like a doll that was sold by Montgomery Ward for Christmas of 1939 for $.23.*

Illustration 110. *Also in the* Patsyette *size and from the early 1940s, is this 9½in (24cm) Amish or "Pennsylvania Dutch" couple. Only the arms and legs are jointed. The hair and eyes are painted and the legs are painted black to the knees to represent shoes and stockings. This pair is part of a series that was dressed in various regional and folk costumes. They are all-original. The girl wears a purple dress with a black shawl and bonnet and a white apron. The boy wears a black cotton suit and black felt hat. He also has a brown curly mohair wig and beard. (The beard is a sign of the married state among the Amish sect.)*

Illustration 111. *9¼in girl in the* Patsyette *size with yellow painted hair and black side-glancing eyes. Only the arms and legs are movable. The molded shoes and stockings are painted blue.*

151

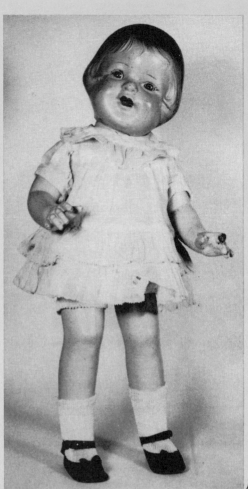

Illustration 112. *19in (48cm) all-composition fully-jointed girl in the* Patsy An[n?] *size with light brown molded hair, blue tin sleep eyes with painted eyelashes onl[y] and an open/closed mouth. She is wearing her original organdy dress in th[e] Patsy-style. The Butler Brothers catalog for October of 1935 showed an almos[t] identical doll that sold for $8.00 a dozen.*

Illustration 113. *For Christmas of 1937, Sears, Roebuck and Co. offered this 11[½] in (29cm) girl for $.25. She is all-composition fully-jointed with reddish hair an[d] blue painted eyes.*

Illustration 114. *Original advertisement from the 1937 Sears, Roebuck and C[o.] Christmas catalog for a doll similar to the one shown in* Illustration 113.

113.

Dainty All-Composition Dolls

Real bargains! Hard-to-break composition turning, tilting heads, inside jointed arms and legs, sprayed enamel finish with winsome expressions in painted eyes. Shipping weight, each, 12 ounces.

9½-In. Baby Doll	9½-In. Topsy Doll	11½-In. Girl
Adorable. Printed, dotted, lacy organdy dress; bonnet, diaper, socks.	Brown color. Three cute pigtails; ribbon bow ties, colorful garments.	Stands alone. Cu[te] lacy, print dres[s,] hair bow, sock[s,] shoes.
49 V 3446 ..25c	49 V 3445 ..25c	49 V 3444 ..25[c]

112.

Illustration 115. *For Christmas of 1944, Sears, Roebuck an[d] Co. offered these 13in (33cm) girls, shown in the origin[al] advertisement in* Illustration 116. *The dolls have mohair wig[s] and blue painted eyes. Their outfits are replacements.*

Illustration 11[6.] *Original adver- tisement from th[e] 1944 Sears, Roebuck and C[o.] Christmas cata- log for dolls simi- lar to thos[e] shown in* Illustra- tion 115.

115.

116.

Illustration 117. 22½in (57cm) all-original girl in the Patsy-style, from 1939, fully-jointed with a slimmer body than the real Patsy dolls, dark brown painted hair, brown painted eyes and an open/closed mouth. Sears, Roebuck and Co. also sold this doll in a black version.

Illustration 118. 13in (33cm) fully-jointed toddler from the late 1930s with a face like the Pasty Baby, a blonde mohair wig over molded unpainted hair, blue sleep eyes with eyelashes and a closed mouth. She wears her original pink print dress under a white apron and has a matching bonnet. This doll, even though she is made of a cheap lighter-weight composition, is in like-new condition.

Illustration 119. This 18½in (47cm) girl almost looks like a genuine Patsy Ann. She has a blonde mohair wig and blue sleep eyes with eyelashes. The arms are both curved and seem to be from the Shirley Temple mold. The clothing is not original.

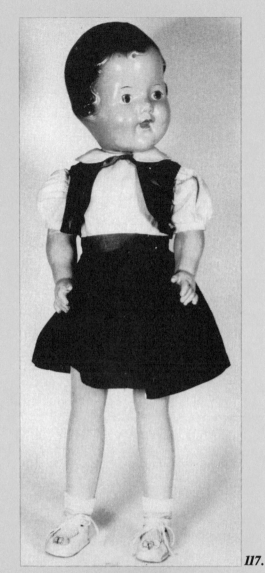

117.

118.

119.

The dolls shown in *Illustrations 120* through *123* also reflect the *Patsy* tradition and are from the 1930s. They are all of superior construction and finishing and are fully-jointed. They all have the "bent" right arm that is typical of the *Patsy* dolls. All of them are unmarked and none of them wear original clothing.

Illustration 121. 19in (48cm) girl with red painted red hair and blue tin sleep eyes with eyelashes.

Illustration 120. 14in (36cm) girl, also with red painted hair and blue tin sleep eyes with eyelashes. The torso, arms and legs are from the same type mold as a genuine marked Patsy.

Illustration 122. *17in (43cm) girl with brown deeply molded painted hair and blue tin sleep eyes with eyelashes. She is marked on the upper right arm at the joint*

ᒧᑕ

and at the upper left arm at the joint

ᒥ4

Illustration 123. *13½in (34cm) girl with red molded painted hair like the Arranbee* Nancy, *seen in* Illustration 97, *blue tin sleep eyes with eyelashes and an open mouth with two upper teeth.*

155

Illustration 124. 8in (20cm) Shirley Temple *paper doll dressed in pajamas and holding a* Patsy *doll. This is Saalfield, number 2112, from 1934.*

Illustration 125. *A still from the 1936 Twentieth Century-Fox film* Captain January. *Shirley Temple is holding a* Patsy Mae. *At the left is Nella Walker, who played Mrs. Mason in the movie.* Photograph Courtesy of Patricia Schoonmaker.

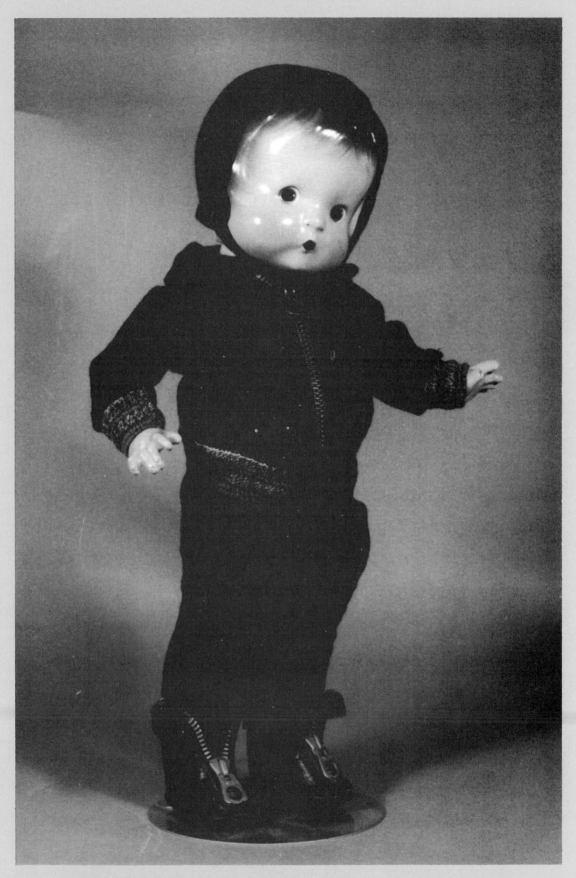

Illustration 126. Patsy *wearing a snowsuit similar to the one shown in the book* Patsy Ann Her Happy Times *by Mona Reed King, seen in* Illustration 15. *This is a red wool two-piece snowsuit with a matching hat. The rubber galoshes also have working zippers.* Rosemary Hanline Collection.

Ideal's *Toni* Dolls, Part I

Illustration 1. *14in (36cm) Toni, waiting for her permanent to "take;" dark brown hair; blue eyes; head marked: "P-90//Ideal Doll//Made in U.S.A.;" back marked: "Ideal Doll//P-90;" original box and Toni Supplies.* Wanda Lodwick Collection.

Back in the late 1940s, the manufacture of composition dolls came to an end after almost a half century of production. This was because of the improvements in synthetic plastics. The almost indestructible "hard plastic" doll was only manufactured by the leading doll companies for about eight years, but during this time some of the most detailed and beautiful dolls ever made in the United States were produced for the mass market.

Synthetic plastics were a perfect material for rendering play dolls. Dolls made from hard plastic had a greater variety of facial expressions and other minute details, such as realistic fingers, than any commercially manufactured dolls made up to that time. The first universally popular hard plastic dolls were Ideal Novelty and Toy Company's

Illustration 2. *15in (38cm) brunette and blonde Tonis, marked: "Ideal Doll//P-91." The shoes on the blonde doll are made of vinyl and marked "Ideal." They are rather awkward looking but these shoes are original and are found on many Toni dolls. Other Tonis wear a more dainty leatherette shoe that snaps in the center at the ankle.*

Toni®, which were first nationally distributed on an extensive basis for Christmas of 1949. The *Toni* doll was sold by the thousands in stores until 1955.

Toni, 27 years old in 1976, was new to the market during the beginning of the Korean War, a time of peak sales and production records. Distributors were alarmed over the possibility of shortages occurring because of the availability of materials and bought and ordered more dolls and toys than could be sold.

In June of 1950, when the United States entered the Korean conflict, there were approximately 42,000,000 children in the country under 15 years of age, a record number. The merchants knew that the "war babies" would need Christmas toys and bought "over their head," fearing government restrictions on strategic materials. Orders of the Ideal Novelty and Toy Company in July of 1950 were 167 percent above what they were in July of 1949. At that time, 2600 workers were busy on Christmas orders; by August more than 3000 were running extra shifts on the assembly lines. The total volume of orders in 1950 for Ideal reached more than $15 million, $4 million above 1949. This is a reason why there are so many *Toni* dolls in doll collections today.

However, "Toni" was a home permanent before it became a doll.

In January of 1948, the Gillette Safety Razor Company bought the Toni Company for $20 million. Toni had earned a staggering $5 million profit the preceding year, so this seemed like a good investment. A college football player, Richard Neison "Wishbone" Harris, began the Toni Company in 1936 by buying the "broken-down" Noma Company, which made hair waving equipment for beauty shops, for $5000. By shrewd advertising, Mr. Harris had cornered more than 50 percent of the home permanent business. The Toni Home Permanent kit sold for $1.25 ($2.00 for the

158

Illustration 3. 14in (36cm) P-90 Toni *with vinyl arms and red painted finger-nails. These arms are also found on Harriet Hubbard Ayer.*

luxe model) at a time when curls at the beauty shop cost from $10 to $50. The name for the permanent was originally planned as "Tony" which, in the slang of the time, meant "classy; high-class; top-rate." "Toni" sounded more appealing.

A cold wave which curled hair chemically for $1.25 was very appealing to millions of women who were used to paying ten times as much for heat-waved hair in beauty salons. Clever advertising, costing $5 million a year, instructed every woman in the country that she needed a Toni.

The slogan "Which Twin Has the Toni?" is still a part of the American colloquial jargon. In a comparative-advertising scheme, magazines carried photographs of identical twins, one of whom had a Toni Home Permanent and the other a beauty parlor job. A twin searching and testing staff was set up under Miss Coralie Shaefer, who interviewed identical females between 14 and 25 who could be photographed to appear in magazines and who would testify over the radio.

By the end of 1948, Toni's share of the home wave market was 86 percent and beauty shop profits were cut by more than 20 percent. In New York, Mississippi, Virginia, South Carolina, California and Wisconsin, beauty shop forces appealed to state legislators to pass a variety of laws to hamstring the use of home waves. Florida beauticians tried to have Toni Home Permanents banned because the waving lotion was considered dangerous; Kentucky operators tried to make the practice of curling hair at home declared illegal because those who gave the permanents were not licensed; in Louisiana the beauty shops hired lobbyists to put in a bill to drive home permanents out of business through the state legislature, promising a payment of $30,000 after Tonis were banned. The professional hair wavers were unsuccessful in their bid to monopolize the market and retaliated only by running specials for "home-ruined hair." The beauticians admitted their defeat when they advertised "Toni Wave Given Professionally" in local newspapers and shop windows.

By 1948, Toni sponsored the popular radio programs "Give and Take," "Ladies Be Seated" and "Don McNeil's Breakfast Club," which were audience-participation shows slanted heavily at women listeners, and the soap opera "This is Nora Drake," making Toni and the Toni slogan a household word.

When *Toni* became a doll by Ideal, her name already had an international reputation. (Toni Home Permanents were also sold in Western Europe.)

So with a doll shortage anticipated and the doll industry expected to suffer a lack of allocations because of the war in Korea, Ideal produced an abundance of *Toni* dolls and pushed sales "like crazy." Their skill in plastics helped to put Ideal out in front. A staff of 150 technicians working the plastic division translated doll ideas into new materials as they became available for *Toni's* hair when shortages were occurring in other types of wig fibers.

Ideal became a leader in American doll production in 1902 when Morris

Illustration 5. 14in (36cm) and 16in (41cm) Toni *walkers. Both have blonde wigs and eye shadow. The smaller doll is marked "P-90" on her head and "90-W" on her back. The larger doll is marked "P-91" on her head and "16" on her back.*

Illustration 4. 14in (36cm) redhead, brunette and blonde *Tonis; marked: "P-90."*

Illustration 6. 20½in (52cm) Toni; platinum hair; eye shadow; marked: "Ideal Doll P-93." The label on the dress reads: "Genuine Toni Doll with Nylon Wig."

Michtom, the founder of the company, gave the teddy bear to the world. This began a new trend towards dolls that could be played with instead of merely looked at, as was the case with dolls that had bisque and china heads, and it came about because in 1902 President Theodore Roosevelt went hunting in Mississippi. One day a cute little bear cub wandered into the camp. "T.R." was too "soft-hearted" to shoot it. A cartoonist made a drawing of the incident and called it "Teddy's Bear."

Mr. Michtom, who operated a toy shop in New York, quickly designed a plush bear and rushed a sample off to the White House along with a letter asking permission to call it "Teddy Bear." "Dear Mr. Michtom," came the prompt reply, "I don't think my name is likely to be worth much in the bear business, but you are welcome to use it."

Ideal Novelty and Toy Company was founded to produce the bears. In 1933, Mr. Michtom hit the biggest doll jackpot ever with another famous name, Shirley Temple. When the first shipment of Shirley Temple dolls arrived in Hollywood by air express, it was met at the airport by an escort of motorcycle police and conducted with

screaming sirens to the store where it went on sale. Other cities reacted with similar, if not such elaborate, enthusiasm. By the time Mr. Michtom, "the Teddy Bear man," died in 1938, sales of the Shirley Temple doll had totaled more than six million dolls. This was back in the Depression when a family could be fed for a week for the cost of a Shirley Temple doll.

Enormous outputs are maintained by fresh new ideas, and Ideal was always an innovator, not a copier. A doll that could be given a home permanent was another of Ideal's major successes.

The chemists of the DuPont Company were enlisted to create a fiber for this doll's hair. Even a new type of glue was developed to hold the hair firmly to the doll's head during her frequent shampoo sessions.

In 1949, the 14in (36cm) size Toni doll sold for $9.95. (This is equal to $23 in December of 1975.) Toni came in a box with the same magenta and gray stripes as the famous Toni Home Permanent kits. She had her own lanolin "creme shampoo," a Toni "play wave" consisting of sugar and water solution, 12 plastic "Midget Spin Curlers," papers for wrapping the hair in the curlers, her own personal comb and, of course, the "Directions for Toni Play Wave."

As a caution to Toni's beautician's "mother," a notice was included stating that the "play wave" was absolutely safe in the hands of children" but they should "NEVER...play with real home permanent waving lotion." A recipe was given to make more Play Wave Lotion: "Mix 1 teaspoon of sugar with 1/3 cup water."

In 11 easy steps with photographs, the little owner was instructed how to give Toni her permanent and then style her hair.

Following these instructions, the procedure requires considerable concentration, dexterity and patience. Even with great care, Toni lost more hair each time she needed a new permanent because the glue holding the wig to her head was not completely non-water-soluble. The Play Wave Instructions had informed the young beauty operator that "The Magic Nylon Wig on your Toni doll is very expensive to make. It's the only kind of doll hair that you can shampoo and wave over and over again and still keep it looking like new. Naturally, the more gently you treat her hair...the prettier it will

stay...so treat it as carefully as yc would your prettiest party dress."

Toni was so popular that she can in several sizes ranging from the eas to-find 14in (36cm) size to the 22½ (57cm) size.

In October of 1950, McCall's mag zine offered the first pattern for add tional outfits for Toni. Pattern No. 15 enabled Toni to be a Cowgirl, comple with boots, fringed skirt, shirt, bole and hat; a Drum Majorette; and Fluf Ruffles in a calico dress and picture ha

By 1951, the very popular Toni d with variations of heads and bodies w also Mary Hartline, Harriet Hubba Ayer, Miss Curity and Betsy McCal □

Illustration 7. 18½in (47cm) Toni w light red hair and eye shadow; marke "Ideal Doll//P-19."

Ideal's *Toni*® Dolls, Part II

Featuring Mary Hartline, Betsy McCall, Miss Curity and Harriet Hubbard Ayer

The *Toni*® doll of 1949 from the Ideal Novelty and Toy Company was a creation of Bernard Lipfert, the doll sculptor who rendered the most popular play dolls the 1930s, such as Effanbee's *Patsy* series, Madame Alexander's *Dionne Quintuplets* and Ideal's *Shirley Temple* dolls. A successful and widely sold doll has always been imitated and copied. Johana Gast Anderson's book, *More Twentieth Century Dolls*, shows a doll manufactured by Pedigree, one of England's leading doll producers, on page 1000, which looks exactly like *Toni*. She is called the *Pin-up* doll with "magic nylon hair" that can

"be shampooed and play-waved with the Pin-up Play Perm outfit."

Pin-up is so identical to *Toni* that it is likely that this doll and similar Canadian dolls were authorized by Ideal, unlike the hard plastic dolls of other leading American manufacturers who copied the shampoo-able hair concept for their dolls. Ideal itself released two other dolls in 1952, utilizing the *Toni* doll mold.

The first of these dolls, which is basically the same as *Toni*, was *Mary Hartline*. The *Mary Hartline* dolls using the *Toni* mold are 15in (38cm) and 22½in (57cm). (A 7¾in (20cm) *Mary*

Hartline doll was also made by Ideal.) *Mary Hartline* has long golden side-parted hair and heavy eye shadow above and below the eyes. She is dressed in a bright red majorette costume with matching underpants, wears gold-trimmed boots and came with a small baton in the original package. A metal barrette holds her hair back.

Mary Hartline was an early television personality. From 1949, when she was 23 years old, until 1956 she was the band leader on a popular children's show "Super Circus," which originated live from Chicago and was presented by ABC on Sunday evenings from 5:00 p.m. to 6:00 p.m. The show featured guest acrobats, animal acts and other circus specialities, announced by ringmaster Claude Kirchner. Providing the comedy were the clown, Cliffy the Tramp; Scampy, the Boy Clown; and Nick Francis, "the Fat Clown."

Now [in 1976] Mary Hartline is the widow of Woolworth Donahue and she lives in elegant Palm Beach, Florida, although she still maintains her membership in the American Federation of Musicians.

Ideal's other new doll for 1952 was *Betsy McCall*®, which used the 14in (36cm) P-90 *Toni* body with a different head.

Betsy McCall originated as a paper doll in the May 1951 issue of *McCall's Magazine* and was drawn by Kay Mor-

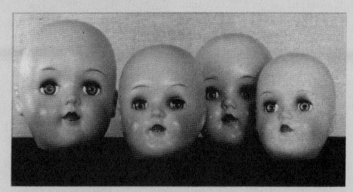

Illustration 8. *The four sizes of marked Ideal heads for the* Toni *doll are, from left to right, the P-93 for the 20½in (52cm) doll, the P-91 for the 15in (38cm) doll, the P-92 for the 18½in (47cm) doll and the P-90 for the 14in (36cm) doll. These heads were available from a doll supply company in the 1950s and were used as replacements for damaged* Toni *dolls and are still "like-brand-new."*

Illustration 10. *The original box for the* Mary Hartline *doll showing the star of "Super Circus" with the doll that represents her.*

York City in the 1880s. Previously sh_ had been a fashionable Chicago societ_ woman but her husband had lost h_ money in bad business investments an_ then had gone through her money an_ afterwards had separated from he_ leaving two daughters in her care. H_ decorating business became more su_ cessful after she accepted a commissio_ to redecorate the yacht of Jame_ Seymour, an oil baron, whom she a_ sumed had become her friend. Mr_ Ayer felt compelled to earn a great de_ of money to regain her former securit_ and so that her daughters would neve_ have to suffer her setbacks.

The older of Harriet Hubbar_ Ayer's daughters married the son of M_ Seymour. By this time, Mrs. Ayer ha_ entered the cosmetics business, her fir_ successful item having been col_ cream, and in a few short years she w_ earning a fortune from this enterpris_ In early 1893, Mrs. Ayer was forcib_ taken to a private mental institutio_ and declared insane. Her now-divorce_ husband and her daughter, Mr_ Seymour, claimed when they had h_ confined that she had become addicte_ to drugs and was incapable of contro_

rissey. At that time, *Betsy* was described as "five, going on six." The *Betsy McCall* paper dolls appeared in the magazine monthly for several years and featured about four new outfits in each issue. In subsequent editions of the full-page series, *Betsy* was joined by her cousins, *Barbara* and *Linda*, and her friend and neighbor, *Jimmy Weeks*, among others.

In September of 1952, *Betsy's* mother took her shopping for a new dress and also promised her a doll. *Betsy*, of course, selected a doll that "looked just like" herself. The *Betsy McCall* page featured paper doll outfits for the new doll that were identical to *Betsy's* own. The same issue of *McCall's* introduced "*Betsy McCall's* new doll," not crediting her to Ideal. This first *Betsy McCall* doll had a vinyl stuffed head with a glued-on dark brown wig and brown round sleepy eyes. This material is an early vinyl called "soft plastic" back then. It has not deteriorated with age and become sticky to the touch as have some forms of vinyl from that era. Her hair could be washed and curled with the accompanying curlers. Also included was a tiny McCall's pattern for a simple apron whose most creative feature was a pocket. McCall's regular patterns 1728 and 1729 featured more outfits for the doll.

Within a few years, *Betsy McCall* dolls had been issued by several of the American doll companies in sizes ranging from 8in (20cm) to 35in (89cm) and some closely resembled the paper doll while others bore little similarity to her.

In time for Christmas of 1953, Ideal marketed two more dolls that were variations of *Toni*.

Miss Curity is the 14in (36cm) P-90 mold and is identical to the same size *Toni* except that her hair is a yellow blonde and she, like *Mary Hartline*, had a liberal application of eye shadow above and below her blue eyes. "The First Lady of First Aid" could also have her hair shampooed and curled with "Ideal's doll curlers."

A "Play Nurse Kit" came with *Miss Curity*. The instructions told how to use the packages of Curity bandages, sterile pads, gauze and absorbent cotton, all products of Bauer and Black, a division of the Kendall Company. Other nursing equipment came in the cardboard suitcase: a tongue depressor, scissors, candy pills, a thermometer, a hypodermic syringe, an eye chart and a fever and temperature chart. These items were so *Miss Curity* could "keep your doll Family healthy." The booklet in the kit told the owner of the doll how "to play nurse" and informed her that for herself, a play nurse's uniform from Ideal was "available now in most department stores."

Ideal's other newcomer in 1953 was *Harriet Hubbard Ayer* who was even more versatile than the other doll characters in the *Toni* line. This doll endorsed a brand of cosmetics named after the founder of the company, a beautiful and stylish New York business-woman of the Gilded Age.

Harriet Hubbard Ayer began her professional career as an interior decorator for the newly wealthy of New

Illustration 9. *Two all original 15_ (38cm)* Mary Hartlines *with the P-_ bodies. The baton seems much too lar_ to be considered as belonging to the d_ but it is original. The white hearts a_ the music notes on the red dresses a_ painted on and are washable.*

Illustration 12. *14in (36cm) all hard plastic* Miss Curity, *marked "P-90" on her head and shoulders. She stands between her original box and the kit containing her nurse supplies. Her uniform is white and her cape is navy blue lined in red.*

Illustration 11. *Ideal's 14in (36cm)* Betsy McCall *doll, marked "P-90" on the shoulders and "McCall Corp." on the vinyl head. Her blouse is white and the jumper is bright red rayon. The apron pattern was included with the doll. Shown on the tag hanging from the doll's left arm is the first* Betsy McCall *paper doll drawn by Kay Morrissey.*

ng her own affairs. The ex-husband nd the daughter both advanced a aim in the courts saying that they ere entitled to manage Mrs. Ayer's roperty, including her lucrative cosetics empire. Harriet Hubbard Ayer ent 14 months in confinement but the ourts saved her company by permitng business associates to manage her ffairs. Mrs. Ayer had appeared in ourt herself in 1889 to accuse her forher client, Mr. Seymour, of attempting o drive her insane. She said that the oil aron was turning robber and that he resaw great profits in her company, hich he planned to control.

The colorful Mrs. Ayer was rescued rom this dilemma and later went on peaking tours to vindicate her characr by relating her experience in the madhouse" to sympathetic audiences.

By the 1950s, the ownership and nanagement of Harriet Hubbard Ayer, ncorporated, had no connection with

Mrs. Ayer or the persons she accused of trying to steal her business. It was this successor company that collaborated with Ideal to produce a doll which used Harriet Hubbard Ayer cosmetics.

The *Harriet Hubbard Ayer* doll came in four *Toni* sizes — 14in (36cm), 15in (38cm), 18½in (47cm) and 20½in (52cm) — and used the standard *Toni* body. Her head, like the one on the *Betsy McCall* doll, is vinyl stuffed with cotton batting and she also has round sleep eyes that open and close independently and a glued-on wig. The color of the hair on different dolls is various shades. Another feature of the *Harriet Hubbard Ayer* doll is vinyl arms with long red fingernails. Her clothing is a gray dress over which she wears a green or red striped apron. □

Toni® is a registered trademark of The Gillette Co.
Betsy McCall® is a registered trademark of McCall Corp.

Illustration 13. *14in (36cm) and 15in (38cm)* Harriet Hubbard Ayer *dolls. Both dresses are gray. The aprons are white with green stripes on the smaller doll and red stripes on the larger one. The vinyl heads are marked "MK 14// Ideal doll" and "MK 16//Ideal doll," although the larger* Harriet Hubbard Ayer *doll, like other dolls using the P-91* Toni *body, is 15in (38cm) tall. The shoes and socks are not original.*

163

A Photographic Essay

One of the greatest advancements in doll manufacturing during the modern era was making dolls of all hard plastic. Plastic is an organic synthetic or processed material that is usually a by-product of petroleum. The first really popular hard plastic doll was IDEAL'S *Toni* who came out in time for Christmas in 1949. *Toni* eventually came in several sizes ranging from 14 in. (35.6cm) to 20½ in. (52.1cm) and the same basic doll was used for other doll characters from IDEAL. The *Toni* doll was an "advertising doll" who had a miniature Toni home permanent kit included with her so that her hair could be curled and set in various styles. The dolls had synthetic nylon, saran or dynel wigs that could be washed and combed without causing permanent damage to them. Durable hard plastic dolls with washable hair were imitated by other doll companies during the 1950s and all sorts of dolls were produced using the concept of the *Toni* dolls.

The following illustrations show the various dolls that utilized the different *Toni* molds from IDEAL. All are dressed in original costumes; some slight variances from originality are pointed out.

The standard head and body molds used for *Toni* dolls are the following with the sizes given for standard versions:

P-90	14 in. (35.6cm)	
P-91	15 in. (38.1cm)	
P-92	18½ in. (47.0cm)	
P-93	20½ in. (52.1cm)	

(Accurate measurements may not coincide with catalog descriptions.)

RIGHT: Illustration 2. Full-page advertisement from a Sunday newspaper supplement from about 1953, showing *Toni, Miss Curity, Harriet Hubbard Ayer* and *Betsy McCall.* The original prices seem surprisingly high even when compared with today's inflationary standards:

Toni	14 in. (35.6cm)	$11.98
	16 in. (40.6cm)	$13.98
	19 in. (48.3cm)	$16.98
	21 in. (53.3cm)	$19.95
Miss Curity	14 in. (35.6cm)	$11.98
Harriet Hubbard Ayer	14 in. (35.6cm)	$11.98
	16 in. (40.6cm)	$13.98
	19 in. (48.3cm)	$16.98
	21 in. (53.3cm)	$19.95
Betsy McCall	14 in. (35.6cm)	$ 7.98

ABOVE: Illustration 1. The four sizes of marked *Toni* doll heads. These were available from a doll supply company in the 1950s to use as replacements for damaged dolls. The heads are marked, from left to right: "P-93 // IDEAL DOLL // MADE IN U.S.A.;" "P-92," same as P-93; "P-91," same as P-93; "P-90," same as P-93.

LEFT: Illustration 3. P-91 *Toni* head with a dark brown replacement wig from the 1950s. The original carton is in the background. (The wig is only resting on the head.) The curlers at the right came attached to the arm of various *Toni* dolls and others of the same type.

ABOVE: Illustration 4. P-90 *Toni* with bright red hair and dark eyeshadow. The back is marked: "IDEAL DOLL // P-90." The original dress is aqua and white.

LEFT: Illustration 5. Two *Toni* walkers with light blonde hair and eyeshadow. Note the walking mechanism which is attached to the head so that it turns from side-to-side when the doll "walks" when led by the arm. The larger doll is 16 in. (40.6cm) tall and has a P-91 head; the back is marked: "IDEAL DOLL // 16." The smaller is 14 in. (35.6cm) tall with a P-90 head; the back is marked: "IDEAL DOLL // 90 W."

RIGHT: Illustration 8. Two P-93 *Tonis*, the largest size. Both are wearing original dresses. The doll on the right has replaced shoes. The dress labels (as on most original Toni clothing) are: "GENUINE TONI DOLL // WITH NYLON WIG // MADE BY IDEAL TOY CORPORATION." The 20½ in. (52.1cm) size is marked on the back: "IDEAL DOLL // P-93."

ABOVE: Illustration 6. Two P-92 Tonis, both with eyeshadow. On the left is a walker with reddish-brown hair, original yellow cotton dress with attached apron; original vinyl shoes marked: "IDEAL TOY CORPORATION // MADE IN U.S.A.;" back is marked: "IDEAL DOLL // 19." On the right is Toni with dark blonde hair and a dress that may not be original. The standard P-92 doll is marked on the back: "IDEAL DOLL // P-19." On the right is Toni with dark blonde hair and a dress that may not be original. The standard P-92 doll is marked on the back: "IDEAL DOLL // P-19."

BELOW: Illustration 7. P-90 and P-91 in ori[ginal] dresses. (The footwear is not original.) The bac[k of] the 15 in. (38.1cm) doll is marked: "ID[EAL] DOLL // P-91."

RIGHT: Illustration 9. P-92 walker. This one is still in her original box that includes a cowgirl outfit and a wedding dress along with extra shoes. The original price was $17.00. This Toni has very light blonde hair and the straw hat is also original. Jean Canaday Collection.

Illustration 10. *Mary Hartline* was first issued in 1952, utilizing the *Toni* mold. She has light blonde hair and dark eyeshadow. The original majorette outfits, copied after those that Mary Hartline wore on the television show "Super Circus," are red cotton with white painting. The original carton and baton belong to the doll on the right. These dolls are the P-91 mold.

Illustration 11. Miss Curity came out for Christmas in 1953. She is the P-90 doll with blonde hair and eyeshadow. All of *Miss Curity's* accessories are shown with the original package. The nurse's uniform is white and the cape is navy blue lined in red.

Illustration 12. *Harriet Hubbard Ayer* is from 1953. On the left is the P-91 body; on the right is the P-90. The stuffed vinyl heads are marked respectively: "MK 16 // IDEAL DOLL" and "MK 14 // IDEAL DOLL." These dolls have hair color of various shades and the wigs are glued to the head. The arms are also vinyl with bright red fingernails. The dresses are gray and the aprons are white with red stripes and white with green stripes. The original ads said that "Harriet Hubbard Ayer is the *only* doll in the world with Ideal's exclusive 'Magic Flesh' —specially made for doll make-up." She had her own "non-staining, washable 8 piece cosmetic kit by Ayer, creator of famous beauty preparations."

Illustration 13A & B. Betsy McCall has the P-90 body and she came out in 1952. The vinyl head has a glued-on dark wig and it is marked: "McCALL CORP." The original costume is a white blouse and a bright red rayon jumper. The McCall's apron pattern came in the original carton that shows a picture of a *Betsy McCall* paper doll which was drawn by Kay Morrissey in McCall's Magazine beginning in May of 1951.

Illustration 14. Shown here is an IDEAL doll called *Sara Ann,* as stated on her original tag. She is identical to the P-90 *Toni* doll and has blonde hair and wears a red and white dress. The vinyl shoes are the later shoes for *Toni* and date the doll from the early to mid 1950s. This doll came in all the *Toni* sizes (thus saving royalties to the Toni Company) and without the original tag is difficult to identify.

Illustration 15. Princess Mary is a very unusual all [...] nal doll on the P-91 *Toni* body from ca. 1954. The [...] is stuffed vinyl and is marked: "IDEAL DOLL // V [...] The hair is an early attempt at "rooted" hair as [...] inserted like the hair on the early wax dolls. The [...] is yellow rayon with an attached slip. Only the s[...] replaced. The doll measures 15¼ in. (38.8cm).

On the left is a 14in (36cm) *Toni*® right out of her original box from about 1951. The head and body are from the P-90 mold and are marked: "IDEAL DOLL." The doll on the right is a 22½in (57cm) *Mary Hartline Toni*-type dolls. The head is a socket head and is only marked: "IDEAL DOLL." The body is marked: "IDEAL DOLL// P-94." She wears a shiny rayon majorette dress.

Toni® is a registered trademark of The Gillette Co.

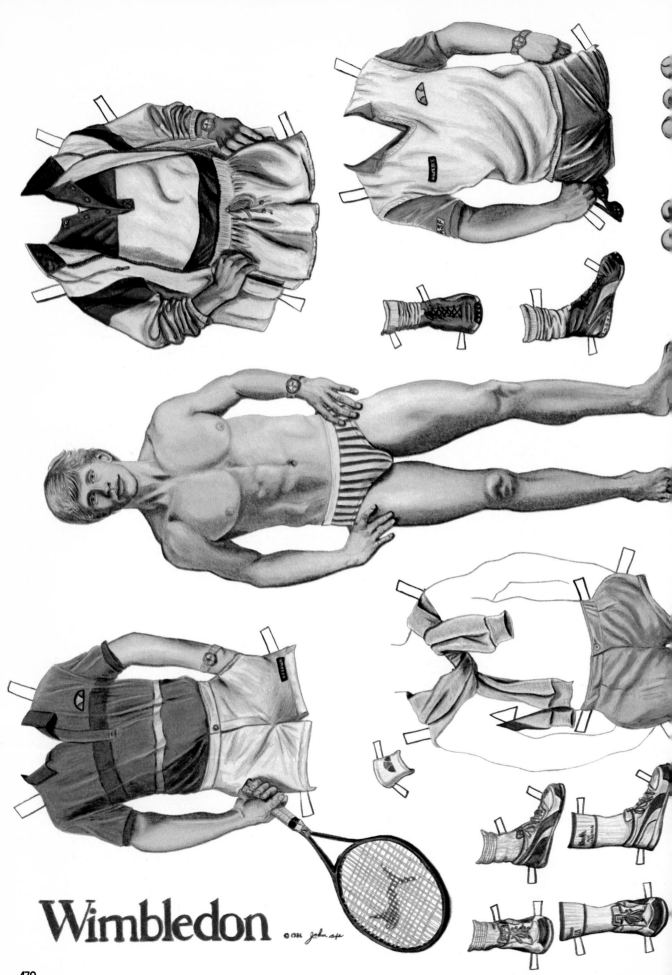

Wimbledon

© 1986 John ...

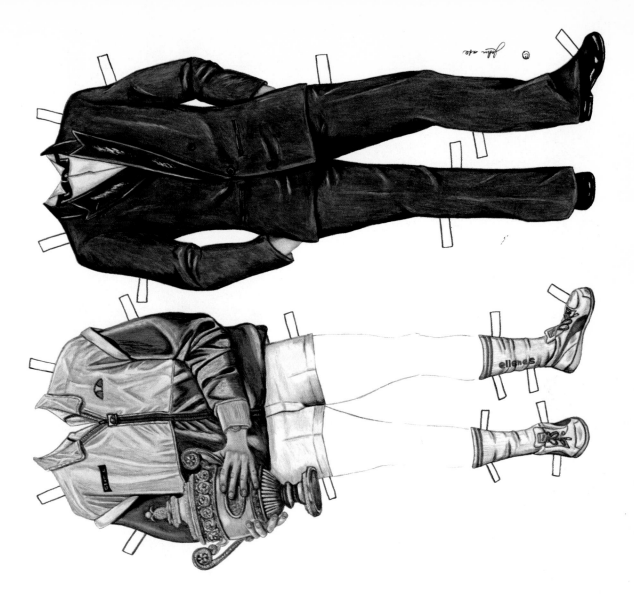

Wimbledon

The All England Tennis Championships held each year at Wimbledon in London are among the world's most prestigious. The matches were inaugurated in 1877 and have been held every year since, with the exception of 1915-1918 and 1940-1945 because of the World Wars. Tennis champions from many different countries all over the world have competed for the coveted Wimbledon cup in Men's Singles and the trophy for Women's Singles. The Wimbledon matches are held on a grass court which can be affected by weather conditions, and members of the All England Club fear that this surface could be replaced by something more durable in the future.

The winners of Wimbledon have become major celebrities with international reputations and they have also earned fortunes from profitable product endorsements. Their equipment and clothing carries the logos of such companies as Adidas and Puma which are seen on television and in magazines all over the world. Several of the winners of the men's singles have been repeat winners. In recent years Rod Laver of Australia has won four times (1961, 1963, 1968 and 1969); John Newcombe of Australia three times (1967, 1970, 1971); Jimmy Connors of the United States twice (1974 and 1982); Björn Borg of Sweden won five times in succession (1976-1980); John McEnroe, and American born in West Germany, three times (1981, 1983, 1984); and Boris Becker of West Germany, the youngest ever at age 17, won twice (1985, 1986).

CHARLIE McCARTHY

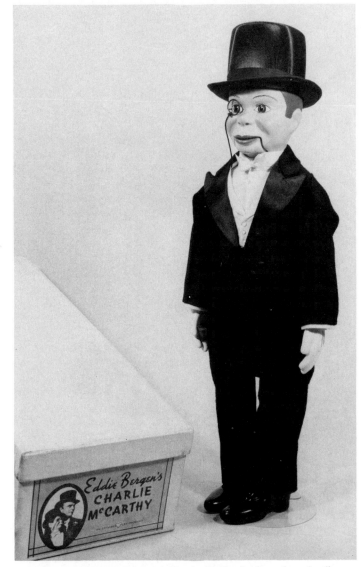

Illustration 1. 1¼in (3.2cm) Charlie McCarthy brass pin painted in realistic colors, 1930s. There is no evidence to show that these pins were attached to the *Charlie McCarthy* dolls. No markings.

In late 1937 Fleischaker & Baum (Effanbee) announced that the company's "biggest scoop of 1938" would be "an exact reproduction of the original Charlie McCarthy made famous by Edgar Bergen." Charlie would be "dressed in his top hat and evening clothes and wearing his monocle."

Charlie McCarthy was a perfect character for play items, as he was so unique and original. In the 1939 Effanbee doll catalog *Charlie McCarthy* with a composition head, hands and feet was advertised in three sizes -- 15in (38.1cm), 17in (43.2cm) and 20in (50.8cm). An all-rubber *Charlie McCarthy* of 9in (22.9cm) had molded features and clothing and was painted with "vegetable coloring."

By late 1938 Ideal Novelty & Toy Co. announced "a new Ideal smash hit," a *Charlie McCarthy* hand dummy to retail for 59¢. The composition head had a molded top hat and a wire monocle. The body portion was cloth with a painted tuxedo.

In the meantime other doll companies rushed out with more economical "ventriloquist dolls" to cash in on the rage for *Charlie McCarthy*. The following lists some of the other ventriloquist dolls from 1938 that are now confused with *Charlie McCarthy* because they have a similar appearance:

Illustration 2. 20in (50.8cm) *Charlie McCarthy* from the color illustration with his original box.

Company	Doll	Description
E. Goldberger	*Gabby Joe*	Sizes of 21in (53.3cm), 28in (71.1cm) and 33in (83.8cm). Retail of $1.00, $1.98 and $2.98. Dressed like the *Charlie McCarthy* detective character. Painted eyes; no monocle.
Uneeda	"Ventriloquist Dolls:" *Elmer* *Ballyhoo Bill* *Talking Tom* *Smart Aleck*	All dressed similar to *Charlie McCarthy*. No monocle.
Regal Doll Corp.	*Willie Talk*	Dressed in a top hat and tuxedo. Looks very similar to *Charlie McCarthy* except that he lacks a monocle.
Natural Doll Co., Inc.	*Tommy Talker*, "The Natural Ventriloquist Doll"	Sizes of 20in (50.8cm), 24in (61cm) and 34in (86.4cm). Retail from 50¢ to $1.98. Looks like *Charlie McCarthy* except for no monocle. "Dressed in assorted costumes including evening clothes, sporting outfit with black coat and checkered pants."

Charlie McCarthy

FROM a limb of hickory to America's best loved character has been the meteoric rise of Edgar Bergen's Charlie McCarthy. Now EFFANBEE offers an *authentic* and *authorized* reproduction of this lovable little rogue.

The EFFANBEE McCarthy dolls have every characteristic of their famous big brother . . . his captivating grin, his hinged jaw (operating from the back) and his indispensable monocle. Made in three sizes and dressed in a wide range of costumes.

	DOZEN
Blue coat, white pants and cap	
15" tall, No. 411	$21.00
20" tall, No. 611	48.00
White coat, white pants and cap	
15" tall, No. 412	21.00
20" tall, No. 612	48.00
White mess jacket, black pants	
15" tall, No. 413	21.00
20" tall, No. 613	48.00
Riding habit and hat	
20" tall, No. 614	48.00
Top hat and tails	
17" tall, No. 520	36.00
Top hat, tails and evening cape	
17" tall, No. 520C	42.00
20" tall, No. 620	66.00
Overcoat, beret and suit	
17" tall, No. 521	36.00
20" tall, No. 621	66.00
Aeroplane luggage with 15" doll and extra clothes	
15" tall, No. T-40	42.00
Wooden steamer trunk with 17" doll and complete McCarthy wardrobe	
17" tall, No. T-4	96.00

No. 310—9" all rubber McCarthy (molded) in top hat and tails—vegetable coloring—$45.00 gross

• 9

REENE ST. • NEW YORK

Illustration 3. Page from the 1939 Effanbee Catalog. Note the great variety of costumes and accessories for *Charlie McCarthy*.

voices were also supplied by Bergen. In 1949 Edgar Bergen and his "dummy" friends went to CBS and were on radio until 1956.

Because of their huge success on radio, Edgar Bergen and *Charlie McCarthy* appeared in about 12 short film comedies for the Vitaphone Company between 1933 and 1935. In 1937 Edgar Bergen received a Special Academy Award "for his outstanding comedy creation, *Charlie McCarthy.*" In 1938 Universal Pictures cast Bergen and *Charlie* in the film *Letter of Introduction,* which was based on the life of Edgar Bergen. This film was so successful that Charlie had his name in the title of *Charlie McCarthy, Detective* in 1939. The popular pair were joined by *Mortimer Snerd* in other films and Bergen also did straight dramatic roles without his dummies. The most notable of these were *I Remember Mama* in 1948 and *The Muppet Movie* in 1979.

Edgar Bergen and *Charlie McCarthy* were among the first top radio stars to appear on television. Their debut was on November 14, 1946, on "Hour Glass," a variety program. From January of 1956 to March of 1957 Bergen and *Charlie* starred on the show "Do You Trust Your Wife?" During this show and on many others on television it could be clearly seen that Edgar Bergen moved his lips when *Charlie McCarthy* spoke. As a ventriloquist, Bergen was not among the best. As a creator of voices and a writer of gag situations he had no equal. The success of Edgar Bergen and *Charlie McCarthy* was based on the fact that their comedy act was so original and clever, and that *Charlie* was so unique in his time. The concept has been imitated ever since.

Charlie McCarthy earned a fortune for Edgar Bergen with his appearances in vaudeville, on the radio, in nightclubs, on

---

In June of 1938 Effanbee issued *W. C. Fields* which was a "ventriloquist doll." This doll was 20½in (52.1cm) and he retailed for $5.95. He had a composition head and a cloth body. A drawstring, like in *Charlie McCarthy,* controlled the mouth for "talking." The doll was dressed in a top hat and tails and was a good likeness of W. C. Fields, the comedy actor in films.

Edgar Bergen, the creator of *Charlie McCarthy,* was born as John Edgar Bergren in Chicago, Illinois, of Swedish parents on September 30, 1903. He died on February 16, 1978. His daughter is the striking blonde model and film star Candice Bergen, born May 8, 1946.

In 1921 Bergen purchased a dummy modeled after the face of an Irish newsboy for $35.00. Bergen had practiced ventriloquism as a youngster and he used the

dummy that he named *Charlie McCarthy* for appearances in vaudeville shows. *Charlie McCarthy* put Edgar Bergen through Northwestern University.

During the 1920s Edgar Bergen and *Charlie McCarthy* appeared in vaudeville and did radio shows with Rudy Vallee. *Charlie's* comedy material was wisecracks, or his reflections of what the average person might think about a given situation but would be afraid to vocalize. This was a new concept in comedy.

From 1937 to 1948 Edgar Bergen and *Charlie McCarthy* had their own highly popular radio show on NBC. The show featured guest stars like Don Ameche and Dorothy Lamour and other characters created by Bergen. These were the hilarious dummy, happy-go-lucky *Mortimer Snerd* and the old maid *Effie Klinker,* whose

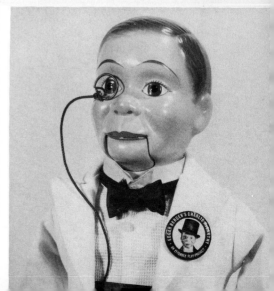

Illustration 4. 15in (38.1cm) *Charlie McCarthy* with the white wool coat. The pin on the lapel is the original pin that Effanbee attached to the dolls.

Charlie McCarthy by Effanbee, circa 1938. The taller *Charlie* is 20in (50.8cm) with a composition shoulder plate head, hands and feet. He has brown painted hair, brown painted eyes and a monocle is attached to the right eye. The body is cloth and can be easily posed in seated positions. The mouth operates with a pull string at the back of the head. This costume is a black silk top hat and a black wool tuxedo with long tails that has satin trim, covered buttons and the coat is lined with satin. The two smaller *Charlie McCarthy* dolls are 15in (38.1cm) and are constructed the same way. Both are missing their hats. The hat that goes with the blue flannel blazer and the white flannel trousers should be a cap, as seen in *Illustration 3*. Marked on the backs of the shoulder plates: "EDGAR BERGEN//CHARLIE McCARTHY//AN//EFFAN-BEE PRODUCT."

television and in the movies. During the late 1930s and the early 1940s there were *Charlie McCarthy* dolls, games, puzzles, paper dolls, coloring books, spoons, tin wind-up toys (the most valuable of all Charlie McCarthy collectibles now) and even Halloween costumes, which added to the money that Bergen's creation earned for him. When Edgar Bergen died in 1978, he bequeathed *Charlie McCarthy* to the Nation. The original *Charlie* is now in the Smithsonian Institution.

ABOVE: Illustration 6. 9in (22.9cm) *Charlie McCarthy* in all-rubber by Effanbee, 1938. The doll is a one-piece construction and is molded and painted. There are no markings. Unfortunately, rubber dolls collapse, harden and crack, as is evidenced here.

ABOVE MIDDLE: Illustration 7. 15in (38.1cm) *Charlie McCarthy* dressed in the blue blazer.

ABOVE RIGHT: Illustration 9. 4in (10.2cm) soap figure of Charlie McCarthy, circa 1939. There are traces of original coloring left.

RIGHT: Illustration 8. 11½in (29.2cm) *Charlie McCarthy* hand dummy by Ideal, 1938. The head is composition with a molded hat and painted features. The cloth glove is black and white paint for trim. Head marked: "CHARLIE//McCARTHY."

Illustration 11. 15½
(39.4cm) Knock-off "Cha[...]
McCarthy" in all-compositi[...]
1940s. Only the head is joint[...]
The doll has a molded a[...]
painted black top hat and s[...]
The marking on the he[...]
indicates the origin and
use of the doll: "CARNEV[...]
(sic) NOV. CO." This [...]
another prize given for winn[...]
a game of chance at carniv[...]
and fairs.

ABOVE: Illustration 10. 15½in (39.4cm) and 10in (25.4cm) "Charlie McCarthy" statues in plaster. The taller Charlie is painted with bright green clothing and probably dates from the 1950s; the smaller figure is in a white suit and probably dates from the 1940s. These items were prizes from carnivals and neither is marked. They are considered "knock-off" items on Charlie McCarthy, although both have the monocle at the right eye.

RIGHT: Illustration 12. 30in (76.2cm) *Charlie McCarthy* from the modern doll era by the Juro Novelty Co., Inc. (a division of E. Goldberger, sometimes called Eegee), 1977. Vinyl head and hands; limp cloth body. The mouth "talks" with a pull string at the back of the head. The monocle is plastic and is embedded into the face. Head marked: "JURO NOVELTY CO. INC.//19 © 77." Still available in retail stores.

Celebrity Dolls

Among the most popular dolls with doll collectors and other collectors of nostalgia are celebrity dolls. And of the celebrity dolls the most desirable seem to be those of entertainment personalities. At the end of 1981 a Lenci doll representing Rudolph Valentino set a new record at an auction. The Valentino doll went for a bid of $4,000,00. At a local auction an 18in (45.7cm) *Shirley Temple* doll in the wrong costume brought $375.00. The vinyl *Shirley Temple* doll from the 1970s is now bringing as much as the 1930s composition one did about 10 years ago. Celebrity dolls are expected to rise even more in value.

My recent book published by Hobby House Press, Inc., is THE ENCYCLOPEDIA OF CELEBRITY DOLLS. I have been researching this project for more than three years. It has been my hobby most of my life. There are many hundreds of celebrity dolls, and establishing their identities is often confusing. The dictionary definition for a celebrity is "a renowned or celebrated person." A celebrity doll then would have to be a doll that represents a famous person. I have confined my research to celebrity dolls that were manufactured commercially, as it would be almost impossible to locate all the dolls that were ever made of famous persons, such as artists' original dolls. My interests focus on the dolls that are more available for collectors.

By tracing the trends and developments in celebrity dolls over the years one can see trends and developments in doll design. Cultural changes are also apparent because

of the sort of doll characters that have been produced. Commercially made dolls reflect public taste and interest. Not all of the most admired celebrities during the eras in which dolls were made commercially were rendered in doll form, but of those who were there are reflections of changing standards in customs and social values. The celebrity dolls themselves are a form of popular history.

Western culture changed immensely during the first decades of the 20th century with the arrival of the movies. The first movies were short films that played in Penny Arcades. The movies gradually became more accepted and moved into places called Kinetoscope Parlors and later into theaters especially built for them. Most of the early films were of a risqué nature and were usually slapstick comedies that appealed to the poor and the young. After the movies began to tell stories they gradually became more accepted as worthy forms of entertainment and also as a form of culture. In 1915 D. W. Griffith's silent classic *The Birth of a Nation* was released. This film was the landmark in motion picture history that caused "respect-

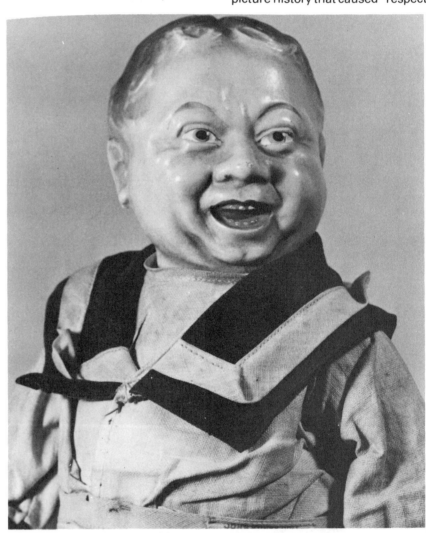

Illustration 1. 13½in (34.3cm) *John Bunny* by Louis Amberg & Son, 1914. Composition head with painted reddish hair and blue eyes; open/closed mouth with painted teeth. The head is marked, but most of the markings are below the wire that holds it on the all-cloth body. Visible is: "© 14." The cloth label on the sailor suit reads:

> JOHN BUNNY DOLL
> COPYRIGHT L. A. & S. 1914 TRADEMARK REGISTERED
> MADE EXCLUSIVELY BY LOUIS AMBERG & SON, N.Y.
> WITH CONSENT OF JOHN BUNNY (name in script)
> THE FAMOUS MOTION PICTURE HERO OF THE VITAGRAPH CO.

The sailor suit is less common than the soldier suit. *Irene Trittschuh Collection.*

Illustration 1. 22in (55.9cm) *Shirley Temple as Heidi* by Ideal, 1937. All-composition and fully-jointed. This very rare original, tagged costume is based on the dream sequence in the film *Heidi,* in which Heidi danced and sang as a Dutch girl. The apron is separate. The hat is white organdy. The wig is also seldom seen on an original composition Shirley Temple doll. It is dark blonde mohair in a center part with bangs and long pigtails gathered up in loops. The cotton stockings are also original, as are the hand-carved wood shoes that are rather thin and fit well to the foot. Head marked: "SHIRLEY TEMPLE." Back marked: SHIRLEY TEMPLE (curved pattern) // 22." *Patricia Slabe Collection.*

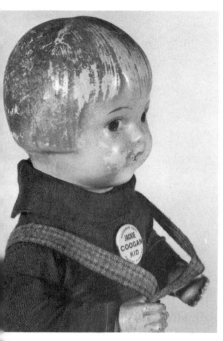

Illustration 2. 13½in (34.3cm) *Jackie Coogan* as *The Kid* by Horsman, 1921. Composition shoulder plate head and arms; cloth body; painted, molded reddish-brown hair; brown painted eyes. The original costume is an aqua shirt and gray pants. Head marked: "E.I.H.Co.//19 © 21." The pin is original. The pants are labeled: "JACKIE COOGAN KID//LICENSED BY JACKIE COOGAN// PATENT PENDING."

able" persons to patronize the movies.

In 1910 a publicity ploy created the first "movie star." It was realized that a recognizable personality was bringing in the customers and the star system was created. Florence Lawrence had the distinction of being the first performer to see her name advertised as a draw for a film. The first big stars were the slapstick comedians who became as familiar to the public as family members. And doll makers got busy making dolls of movie stars.

Most celebrity dolls, but not all by any means, are dolls of entertainment personalities. Celebrity dolls were also made of baseball, basketball, football and hockey players. They were made of political candidates and office holders. They were made of "heroes" and other people of notable achievement. They were made of military men, patriots, Indian leaders, civic leaders, writers, royalty, personalities from history and famous babies and children who never did anything exceptional.

The greatest majority of celebrity dolls were made during the 20th century. This time period was well into the industrial era when dolls and other playthings could be manufactured on a large scale, and many of these items have survived to become collectible. The following shows some of the trends that celebrity dolls have taken during each decade of the 20th century. Only a small sample of the dolls from each period is cited.

1900 to 1910. One of the greatest events of the decade was the "discovery" of the North Pole. Robert E. Peary reached the North Pole on April 6, 1909. Frederick A. Cook then insisted that he had done this in 1908, but his trip was later discredited. Peary's little daughter, Marie Ahnightio, was claimed to have been the first white child born north of the Arctic Circle (1893). This certainly is not true, but it made good publicity for Peary. By the fall of 1909 several doll companies began advertising dolls of *Cook*, *Peary* and Peary's daughter, *The Snow Baby*. These were bisque-headed dolls who had jointed composition bodies covered with real fur. The voyages to the north also drew attention to the natives there, so many "Eskimo" dolls were also advertised by various companies, such as Strobel & Wilken.

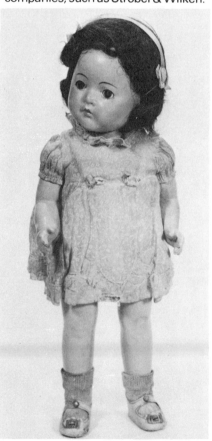

Illustration 3. 17½in (44.5cm) *Yvonne Dionne* girl by Madame Alexander, circa 1939. Dark brown human hair wig; brown sleep eyes with lashes; closed mouth; composition shoulder plate head, arms and legs; tightly stuffed cloth body with a cryer inside. Head marked: "ALEXANDER." *Rodolfos Collection.*

1910 to 1920. Adult male actors in silent film comedies were easily recognizable persons by this time and became popular in doll form. The first doll of a movie star was of

Illustration 4. 16in (40.6cm) *Prince Edward, the Duke of Kent* by Chad Valley, 1953. Pressed felt head with inset blue glass eyes; blonde mohair wig. The body is fully-jointed of stuffed cotton velvet. The doll is marked with a label attached to the sole of the right foot and was made in England. This doll was originally produced in 1938. The doll shown was manufactured by special request in 1953. *Shirley Buchholz Collection.*

Augustus Carney as *Alkali Ike* in 1913 by the Essanay Film Mfg. Co. Carney played Alkali Ike in a series of rustic comedies and was immensely popular from 1909 to 1913. In 1914 John Bunny, who appeared in more than 200 short comedies between 1910 and 1915, was made as the *John Bunny* doll by Louis Amberg and Son. In 1915 Amberg and other companies began making *Charlie Chaplin* dolls. Charlie Chaplin was the most popular comic of the era and the first to become a millionaire by acting in the movies. These dolls had composition heads and jointed cloth bodies.

1920 to 1930. Child actors in films were sure to appeal to children as dolls. The first child star to be made as a doll was *Jackie Coogan* by Horsman in 1921. Jackie Coogan became an international celebrity after playing a bright-eyed ragamuffin in Chaplin's first feature length film *The Kid* in 1921. The *Jackie Coogan* doll had a durable composition head. Baby Peggy was also a popular child performer in silent films, some of which were remade later in sound with Shirley Temple. Louis Amberg & Son began manufacturing *Baby Peggy* dolls with composition heads and imported bisque heads from Germany by 1923.

The hero of the decade, Charles Lindbergh, flew non-stop from New York to Paris in 1927. The Regal Doll Company commemorated this event with a composition head doll in 1928. The doll was called *Our Lindy.*

1930 to 1940. This was *the* era of celebrated children in doll form. It began with the all-composition *Shirley Temple* doll, the most popular celebrity doll of all time, by Ideal in 1934. Effanbee also brought out composition *Anne Shirley* child dolls that year. This character was based on the lead in the film *Anne of Green Gables* and various Effanbee dolls were used for the earliest *Anne Shirleys*, such as *Mary Lee, Patricia Kin, Patricia* and dolls that were marked "ANNE-SHIRLEY." Madame Alexander presented her child star, *Baby Jane,* in 1935. That same year she introduced the most famous babies in the world, the *Dionne Quintuplets,* as dolls. These are still the largest variety of celebrity dolls of all time. There are 35 different sets of the five dolls, and among the 35 sets there are several different types of costumes. Most of the dolls are made with composition parts but several sets are all-cloth. By the end of the decade other celebrated children were presented as dolls. Among these are *Princess Elizabeth* and *Jane Withers* in 1937 by Alexander and *Baby Sandy* in 1939 by Ralph A.

Illustration 5. 7¾ in (19.8cm) *Laurence Harvey as Romeo* and *Susan Shentall as Juliet* by Madame Alexander, No. 474 and No. 473, 1955. All-hard plastic and fully-jointed; straight-leg walkers. He has a red caracul wig and she has a blonde synthetic wig; both have blue sleep eyes with molded lashes. Backs marked: "ALEX." Costumes tagged "ALEXANDERKINS." *Patricia Gardner Collection.*

Illustration 6. 18in (45.7cm) *Haleloke* by Cast Distributing Corp., early 1950s. All-hard plastic and fully-jointed walker; black Saran wig; blue sleep eyes; open mouth with teeth. The trunk set includes extra Hawaiian costumes. Back marked: "MADE IN U.S.A." *Fran's Dolls.*

Illustration 7. 21in (53.3cm) Bob Keeshan *Captain Kangaroo* by Baby Barry Toy, la 1950s. Vinyl head and hands; stuffed clo body; gray painted hair and moustache; bl set-in glass eyes. The black vinyl feet are part the body construction. Marked on the nec " © //B.B.' Tag on clothing "EXCLUSIY LICENSEE//BABY BARRY//TOY N.Y.C Reverse of tag: "CAPTAIN//KANGAROC *Wanda Lodwick Collection.*

Freundlich, Inc. All of them were in composition.

When George VI was crowned King of England in 1937 the ceremony included the participation of the little princesses, Elizabeth and Margaret Rose. This brought attention to royal children and they became celebrities who were popular figures for doll makers. The most notable of the dolls made of *Princess Elizabeth* and *Princess Margaret*

Rose were those in felt by Chad Valley in 1938. There were also dolls of *Prince Edward, the Duke of Kent,* and his sister *Princess Alexandria,* both of whom were cousins of the daughters of George VI.

1940 to 1950. This decade was *the* era of teen and adult movie stars in doll form. During the Depression of the 1930s the movies were doing good business by providing escapist

Illustration 8. 7¼in (18.5cm) (Fischer) *Quintuplets* by Madame Alexander, 1964. Hard plastic heads with sprayed brown hair and blue sleep eyes with molded lashes; jointed vinyl bodies. These dolls are never marked. The original sweaters are labeled: "MFR of the//"ORIGINAL QUINTUPLETS"//by MADAME ALEXANDER." The white cotton nightgowns hanging in the center rear have the same labels. The two different pillow and blanket sets in the boxes were also sold for the "Original Quintuplets." They were boxed in sets of six, to be sold individually in retail stores.

are for those wishing to be entertained. The year 1939 was the greatest of all in the history of Hollywood films. That was the year of such classics as *Gone With the Wind*, *Stagecoach*, *Mr. Smith Goes to Washington*, *Wuthering Heights*, *Of Mice and Men*, *Gunga Din*, *The Hunchback of Notre Dame* and *The Wizard of Oz*.

Ideal had begun producing dolls of *Deanna Durbin*, one of the biggest stars of the late 1930s and the 1940s in 1938. In 1939 Ideal made the Judy Garland as *Dorothy* from *The Wizard of Oz* and Madame Alexander began her dolls of top star *Sonja Henie*. Effanbee was continuing its *Anne Shirley* lady dolls. By August 1940 Madame Alexander was advertising her Vivien Leigh as *Scarlett O'Hara* from *Gone With the Wind* in several sizes. *Sabu* was made by Molly-'es in 1940 and Ideal had a *Judy Garland* teen doll in 1941. These dolls were all-composition.

The most popular child star of the 1940s was Margaret O'Brien. In 1946 Alexander made an all-composition *Margaret O'Brien* doll. This was the last popular celebrity doll in composition. It was also the first celebrity doll in all-hard plastic in 1947. By the end of the 1940s there were very few composition dolls being made, as hard plastic had become the most popular medium for making play dolls.

1950 to 1960. The decade of the 1950s began with celebrity dolls in hard plastic and ended with celebrity dolls in vinyl. Hard plastic permitted more detailing in the faces of the dolls, but very few dolls were produced that were actually "portraits" of the celebrities.

Entertainment personalities continued to be the most popular celebrities in doll form. Alexander made

Mary Martin in 1949 and 1950 from her role on Broadway in *South Pacific*. At about the same time Alexander produced *Piper Laurie*, a starlet in films. Television performers were also made in doll form. An unknown company made *Roxanne* from "Beat the Clock" in 1952; Ideal had *Mary Hartline* from "Super Circus" the same year; The Roberta Doll Company had *Lu Ann Simms* from "Arthur Godfrey and His Friends" in about 1953; the Star Doll Company had *Dorothy Collins* of "Your Hit Parade" in 1954. One of the last dolls in all-hard plastic was *Shari Lewis* from her television

Illustration 9. 36in (91.4cm) *Lori Martin as Velvet Brown* from "National Velvet" by Ideal, 1961. Vinyl head with rooted dark brown hair; the remainder is plastic; fully-jointed with a twist waist and twist ankles; blue sleep eyes with lashes. The original boots are made of vinyl. Head marked: "METRO GOLDWYN MAYER INC.//MFG//IDEAL TOY CORP.//38." Back marked: "© IDEAL TOY CORP.//G-38." The cloth tag also tells that the character is copyrighted by Metro, Goldwyn Mayer Inc. (Some *Lori Martin* dolls measure 38in (96.5cm). *Barbara DeVault Collection*.

Illustration 10. 12in (30.5cm) *Joe Namath* by Mego, 1970. Soft vinyl head; remainder hard vinyl; painted hair and features; fully-jointed. ""BROADWAY JOE" TM// © MEGO CORP. MCMLXX//MADE IN HONG KONG." In the original package the doll was dressed in a football outfit. This suit is an extra outfit for *Joe Namath* from Mego.

shows for children by Madame Alexander in 1959. This was one of the few dolls for which an attempt at portraiture was made.

The year 1957 brought a change in materials and the return of a great favorite. Ideal made a new series of *Shirley Temple* dolls in vinyl with rooted hair. By the end of the decade there were vinyl-headed dolls of circus clown *Emmett Kelly*, singer *Elvis Presley* and children's entertainer on television *Pinky Lee*, among others.

1960 to 1970. By the 1960s there was a great increase in diversity of types among celebrity dolls. They were no longer mostly child performers and lovely actresses. All of the dolls now had vinyl heads and most of them had rooted hair.

From television there was Donna Douglas as *Elly May* from "The Beverly Hillbillies" from an unknown manufacturer, *Patty Duke* by Horsman, Anne Francis as "Honey West" by Gilbert, Barbara Eden of "I Dream of Jeannie" (as *Jeannie*) by Libby and many other lady dolls. Dolls were also made of male stars. There was Vincent Edwards as *Dr. Ben Casey* from "Ben Casey," Richard Chamberlain as *Dr. Kildare* from "Dr. Kildare," Robert Vaughn as *Napoleon Solo* from "The Man from U.N.C.L.E.," and many others.

From the movies there was Sean Connery as *James Bond* by Gilbert, Julie Andrews from *The Sound of Music* and *Mary Poppins* by different companies in different materials (plastic and vinyl combinations), *Laurel* and *Hardy* from their old films on television, and several other adult characters.

Political figures were made as dolls. There was *President Kennedy, Premier Nikita Khurshchev, Lyndon B. Johnson* and *Barry Goldwater.*

Singing groups were presented as small dolls by various companies. Among them were *The Mamas and the Papas, The Beatles, The Dave*

come Back, Kotter;" four dolls from "Happy Days;" and others.

2. Shindana produced dolls of black performers. Among them were *Rodney Allen Rippy, Flip Wilson, Redd Foxx, Marla Gibbs, O.J. Simpson, Jimmie Walker* and *Julius "Dr. J." Irving.* Unfortunately, Shindana is now out of business.

3. The Bicentennial year, 1976, saw "The Heroes of the American Revolution," the Hallmark series of famous Americans and the first six *First Ladies* by Madame Alexander. At the present rate of production the entire *First Ladies* set by Alexander will not be complete

Illustration 11. 21in (53.3cm) Jimmie Walker a *Talking J. J.* from "Good Times" by Shindan 1975. All-printed cloth. The pull ring mak J. J. say phrases like his famous reactio "Dyn-o-mite." Tag: " © 1975//TANDEM PRODUCTIONS//INC.//SHINDANA TOYS Sewn skin made in Taiwan; doll made in th United States.

Illustration 12. 6¾in (17.2cm) *P. T. Barnum* by Hallmark, No. 400DT113-9, 1979. All-cloth with printed clothing and features. Copyright by Hallmark Cards, Inc., August 1979. Made in Taiwan.

Clark Five, The Monkees and *The Spencer Davis Group.*

Madame Alexander made several dolls who were not advertised as celebrities, but everyone knew whom the dolls represented. These were *Jacqueline* and *Caroline* (Kennedy), (Fischer) *Quintuplets* and *Leslie* (Uggams).

1970 to 1980. This decade saw the largest diversity of celebrity dolls ever and several new trends in doll making. Most of the dolls continued to be made of vinyl, which will probably become the longest continually produced material for play dolls of all time. There are six definite trends:

1. Television star dolls produced in sets. There were Penny Marshall and Cindy Williams as *Laverne* and *Shirley; Charlie's Angels,* four dolls from three companies (Hasbro, Mego and Mattel); *KISS*--four bizarre male musicians in Kabuki makeup; six dolls from "The Waltons;" five dolls from "Wel-

until almost the end of the 20th century.

4. Nostalgia. There were dolls of *The Wizard of Oz* stars from the 1939 movie; *Our Gang* child stars from the 1930s; *Shirley Temple,* for the third time; and *Charlie Chaplin* again.

5. Dolls made for boys. There were *Shaun Cassidy* and *Parker Stevenson* as *The Hardy Boys.* There were large sets of dolls from science fiction movies and television shows. Among them are *Star Wars, Star Trek, Buck Rogers in the 25th Century, The Black Hole,* and *Battlestar Galactica.* These dolls came in sets of two different sizes, about 12in (30.5cm) and about 3 3/4in

Illustration 13. 7¾in (19.8cm) *Charlie Chaplin* by Peggy Nisbet, No. P755, 1970s. All-plastic with jointed arms; black painted hair and blue painted eyes; wood cane and cloth rose. Made in England.

(9.6cm). There are so many different sets of the smaller dolls, or "action figures," that they will certainly become hot collectibles in the future.

6. Dolls made especially for collectors. Peggy Nisbet dolls include all the types of celebrity dolls mentioned, featuring dolls of royal persons. These are made in England, as are Ann Parker dolls. The Ann Parker dolls concentrate on "English characters and costumes." Many of the American commercial companies began producing dolls especially for collectors, with Effanbee taking the lead with its Limited Edition Doll Club, which presented the Dewees Cochran self-portrait doll.

1980 and Beyond. The trends from the 1970s are continuing. Ideal is making 12 different Shirley Temple dolls. New companies are making dolls especially for collectors. Effanbee is in the lead with the most artistic and realistic celebrity dolls ever produced by a commercial company. The *W.C. Fields, John Wayne* and *Mae West* dolls were collectible even before they were available for sale.

Celebrity dolls will always be collected and they will always be desirable dolls. They are "someone," not just a doll with an ambiguous name and identity.

Illustration 14. 12in (30.5cm) Harrison Ford as *Indiana Jones* from *Raiders of the Lost Ark* by Kenner, No. 46000, 1981. All-vinyl and fully-jointed; brown painted hair; blue painted eyes. Head marked: " © G.M.F.G.I. 1979." Back marked: "©G.M.F.G.I. 1978 KENNER PROD.//CINCINNATI, OHIO 44512//MADE IN HONG KONG." This is the same doll as Harrison Ford as *Han Solo* from *Star Wars* in 1979 except that the *Han Solo* has brown painted eyes.

CAPTAIN STUBING

Illustration 15. 3¾in (9.6cm) Gavin MacLeod as *Captain Stubing* from "The Love Boat" by Mego, No. 23005/1, 1982. All-vinyl and fully-jointed; painted fringe of gray hair; painted features; molded clothing. Copyright by Aaron Spelling Productions, Inc. Made in Hong Kong.

All of the *Anne Shirleys*

Imagine the surprise I experienced recently [in 1976] when I answered the telephone and the voice on the other end said, "This is Anne Shirley."

The call was in response to a letter I had written. I had hoped that it would reach her but I did not anticipate such results! Anne Shirley, who was one of Hollywood's top film stars of the 1930s and the 1940s, retired from an active life in the movie industry in 1944 at the age of 25 when she was a major box office success and she has not appeared in a film since. The telephone call was not out of character for Anne Shirley. At the peak of her popularity, according to those who worked with her, she exhibited this same warmth and generosity which many of her colleagues lost as their careers developed.

Anne Shirley is remembered today as one of the most popular child actresses in an age of many famous child stars. She is also one of the very few child stars who made the successful transition to adult roles. Her films are shown on television today but her fame is carried into the present generation even more visibly because she was immortalized as one of the Effanbee's most popular dolls.

Overnight success and whimsical publicity campaigns did not create Anne Shirley's career. Her professional life began in New York City, where she was born Dawn Evelyeen Paris in 1919. As a professional photographer's model, she supported her divorced mother when she was only 18 months old. When she was three and a half years old, she appeared under the name Dawn O'Day in Fox and Paramount films made in New York. Alan Dwan, who later directed Shirley Temple in *Heidi* and *Rebecca of Sunnybrook Farm*, advised her mother to take Baby Dawn to Hollywood. This was in 1923. She appeared in about 50 silent films and early talkies as Dawn O'Day, playing such roles as the youn-

Illustration 1. *Anne Shirley in 1938. This portrait was an endorsement for Longines-Wittnauer watches.*

ger Jean Arthur, Madge Bellamy, Frances Dee, Ann Dvorak, Janet Gaynor, Myrna Loy, Barbara Stanwyck and Fay Wray, which in itself sets a record. This new career lasted until she was 15 years old. She was kept so busy portraying children on the screen that she missed her own childhood completely. Her early education was acquired on the set from studio tutors. Even though she escaped the "awkward age" of child performers, work in films was becoming increasingly difficult to obtain as she grew older. She had spent most of her life acting in movies but she gradually became an "unknown."

In 1934, she was "discovered" again when George Nicholas, Jr., was hired

to direct *Anne of Green Gables* for RKO. He insisted on Dawn O'Day whom he remembered in various child parts, for the lead role. When the contract was drawn up, she had to take the name Anne Shirley as part of "getting the job." Anne Shirley was the name of the heroine in the story.

Anne of Green Gables opened during the Christmas season of 1934 and was hailed as a critical success. The film was based on the famous children's novel by Canadian author L. M. Montgomery. The story is set on Prince Edward Island and it describes the arrival of a gangling pigtailed orphan girl at the village of Avonlea and of her adoption by a lonely middle-aged couple. The movie depicts Anne Shirley as a poor but philosophical young girl who goes off to school and acquires her first beau (played by Tom Brown, who was also the lead in *Tom Brown's School Days*). She encounters a series of delightful incidents which become unbelievably important as Anne reports them.

Now, as Anne Shirley, she also starred in *Anne of Windy Poplars*, the sequel to this film, in 1940, and, although it was not as well received, in the meantime she had attained major stardom as Anne Shirley and appeared in many other successful movies such as *Stella Dallas* (1937) with Barbara Stanwyck and *Saturday's Children* (1940) with Dick Powell and Claire Trevor, making the graceful transition to adult roles. She was a Hollywood phenomenon who was loved and respected by all who knew her and she was content with the career her mother had wanted for her.

Miss Shirley says today, "I did everything the studio said. I was company owned and happy about it. I was paid well for my services and I had a good steady job." This was during the Depression and in an age of ironclad studio contracts. Many of her fellow performers did not feel the same way, thinking first of what they had to gain in the future. Anne Shirley's future was to walk away from the studio for which she was a loyal performer while under contract, never to return.

This was ten years after she had become Anne Shirley and while she was at the very top.

Today, one of the most highly prized collectibles is the doll that represents the beloved child and adult star. Effanbee produced thousands and thousands of beautiful dolls in the 1930s and 1940s that are embossed with the name "Anne Shirley."

The first *Anne Shirley* doll came out in 1935 in a 14½in (37cm) size. This doll is marked "Effanbee Patricia" on her back. She was dressed as Anne of Green Gables and had brown or green sleep eyes, long red pigtails of human hair or mohair and wore a straw hat or a tam that matched her dress. By 1937, a new 14in (36cm) *Anne of Green Gables*, marked "F & B" on her head, was produced. Both dolls are all-composition, fully-jointed and similar in appearance.

Movies stars in the 1930s and the 1940s endorsed a wide variety of prod-

Illustration 2. *21in (53cm) and 15in (38cm)* Anne Shirleys; *marked "Effanbee//Anne Shirley;" all-composition with brown sleep eyes; replaced clothing and wigs. The larger doll attests to the "Durability" of Effanbee dolls. She was rescued from an extremely damp basement which caused extensive crazing and bubbling to the paint finish but the damage was minimized with liberal applications of machine oil.*

ucts, the most popular items for child stars being dolls and toys. Some film stars amassed a fortune in royalties from these sales, often surpassing the amount paid for their movie roles. Anne Shirley was not so lucky. Effanbee made arrangements directly with RKO, who had given her the name to which it owned the rights. Anne Shirley says, "I had no thought of money for the dolls. I still have the **one** doll that I was given." This is the *Anne of Green Gables* in her straw hat and red braids.

By 1939, Effanbee was mass-producing several different dolls that are marked "Effanbee" with "Anne Shirley" underneath across their backs. The all-composition dolls are ones that were meant to represent Anne Shirley. These dolls are of a high quality construction with thick layers of a durable paint finish. They have rather large hands so that the fingers could be sepa-

Illustration 3. *14½in (37cm) Effanbee Patricia; all-composition with a red mohair wig and brown sleep eyes; original labeled Effanbee clothing and heart bracelet; purchased in 1935 in a package marked: "Anne of Green Gables."* Patricia Slabe Collection.

Illustration 4. *A scene from the 1934 RKO film* Anne of Green Gables *starring Anne Shirley. On the right is Gertrude Messinger as Diana.*

rate. They range in size from 15in (38cm) to 21in (53cm).

Dolls marked "Anne Shirley" were also sold as the *Dewees Cochran American Children* (with four different types of heads); the *Historical Doll* Series (the *Anne Shirley* head with painted eyes rather than sleep eyes); the *Ice Queen* (open mouth with teeth); and the *Little Lady* dolls. This last group also has the *Anne Shirley* head. These dolls were sold wearing many different outfits, most of them rather elaborate, and they had wigs that were usually human hair. The arms, with the same individual fingers, were cast of hard rubber, which does not craze, but is otherwise the same in appearance as the composition body. Some *Little Ladies* had magnets embedded in their palms so they could hold metal objects. This practice was an innovation of the F.A.O. Schwarz Company of New York City. Always a high quality estab-

lishment, Schwarz requested that manufacturers provide them with something "extra" which differed from the regular line of dolls.

After 1941, *Little Lady* dolls were produced in an 18in (46cm) size from new molds. They are just like the *Anne Shirley* dolls except that they are marked "EffanBee//Made in U.S.A." and are all-composition with a thinner and less glossy paint finish than the earlier version.

Most of the composition *Anne Shirley* and *Little Lady* dolls wore a gold-colored metal heart on a chain on their right arms saying "EffanBee Durable Dolls" on both sides.

Between 1949 and 1955, Effanbee produced a large collection of dolls named *Honey*. This was during the time that mass-produced dolls were manufactured from hard plastic. *Honey* came in sizes of 13½in (34cm), 15½in (39cm) and 18in (46cm), including

"walking" versions, and is very similar in appearance to the *Anne Shirley* doll. At the same time, a 27in (69cm) doll made of composition and marked "EffanBee" on the head appeared. She looks just like the earlier *Anne Shirley*, but has bright yellow saran hair and was called *Formal Honey*.

Honey also appeared dressed in fashions created by Elsa Schiaparelli, the Italian designer whose collections received worldwide attention during the 1950s. In hard plastic with jointed ankles and knees, *Honey* was also a ballerina and an ice skater.

In the late 1950s, doll construction gave way to vinyl, a material that could be produced more cheaply. As new Effanbee models appeared, the 20-year tradition of producing carefully detailed dolls dressed in elaborate materials with fancy hairdos, and all inspired by the first *Anne Shirley* dolls, disappeared. □

More about Anne Shirley

Illustration 1. *18in (46cm) Effanbee Historical Doll representing the Civil War Period; marked "Effanbee//Anne Shirley;" all-composition with a brown human hair wig and blue painted eyes; all-original clothing and heart bracelet.*

It seems that almost any doll collection is just the beginning of the whole collection. A doll collection is seldom "complete." That is the fun of it. Some collectors are able to maintain a strict ruthlessness in their acquisitions and will concentrate on a more limited scope. Most of us continue going off in several directions at the same time although we have our "specialties." Soon we find that the dolls themselves are the nucleus of our collection and that all sorts of other things radiate out from them.

We hunger for information. We have the need to learn everything possible about our collections. We guard with pride all the treasures relating to the collection. In honor of the dolls, we have books, photographs, advertising data, dishes, spoons, furniture, toys and all sorts of doll-related items. The dolls are always the "real" collection and all the other things are secondary, yet we cannot resist them. A spoon collector would never want a *Charlie McCarthy* doll, but doll collectors would want Campbell Kid spoons. If the dolls represent famous product-oriented material, such as the *Betsy McCall®* dolls, there are many variations because of dolls produced by several manufacturers, not to mention other Betsy McCall collectibles. There are Kewpie items galore. With celebrity dolls, there is a wealth of things relating to the dolls. There are children's novels, paper dolls, clothing, tablets, mirrors and a great variety of usable commodities on which the personality could be depicted.

The variations in celebrity dolls alone are endless. Who can resist another example of a doll that is different than those we have already? No matter how many we collect, new ones keep appearing to excite our collecting passion — and to keep us broke.

In view of the interest in Anne Shirley and the *Anne Shirley* dolls, more *Anne Shirley* dolls in different variations, with original outfits and with hair in original sets are shown here which can serve as aids to collectors of these dolls. Even beginning collectors should strive to have their dolls looking as original as possible, an easily achieved accomplishment.

Illustration 2. 21in all-original Effanbee Anne Shirley Little Ladies; *all composition with hard rubber arms; red-blonde human hair wigs, blue sleep eyes. Note the magnetic features of the hands of the doll on the right.*

The *Anne Shirley* composition dolls manufactured by Effanbee from 1935 to the early 1950s fall into the following categories:

Marked *Patricia*, dressed as *Anne of Green Gables*.

Marked *Anne Shirley*, in all-composition.

Marked *Anne Shirley*, all-composition with painted eyes; used for the *Historical Doll* series.

Marked *Anne Shirley* bodies with different heads; the two types are Dewees Cochran's *American Children* series and the *Ice Queen*, a doll dressed in a skating outfit; some of these dolls have open mouths and teeth.

Little Lady marked *Anne Shirley*; arms are manufactured of hard rubber which looks just like composition but is more durable and permits finer detail.

Little Ladies marked only "EFFanBEE," in all-composition.

All-composition marked *Suzanne*.

Honey, marked only "EFFanBEE," in all-composition; later manufactured in hard plastic.

Variations in these groupings may occur. Wig materials of mohair, human hair, saran or yarn floss appear on the same type dolls. There are different hairdos and various shades of hair coloring. Within the same group there are size differences. All of these dolls except *Patricia* and *Suzanne* usually have large hands with completely separated fingers. The *Patricia* doll was the first to be dressed as Anne Shirley from the movie *Anne of Green Gables*. *Suzanne* has the same head modeling as marked *Anne Shirley* dolls, although she is smaller in size. Some *Anne Shirley* dolls and *Little Lady* dolls have black hair and dark skin coloring to represent persons of African descent.

Fans of the *Anne Shirley* dolls have become, or always were, fans of Anne Shirley, one of the most beloved film stars of the 1930s and the early 1940s. Although she never received singular attention for her unique talent in the form of a major award presentation, Anne Shirley usually fared well with film critics. She was well trained, having begun her career in the movies in 1923 as the child actress Dawn O'Day. As Anne Shirley, she was a headliner after her first starring role in *Anne of Green Gables* in 1934.

Even in minor productions, such as *Girls' School*, a forgotten 1938 drama, special mention was made of Anne Shirley's competence by critics. *Steamboat Round the Bend* was one of Will Rogers' last films and was released after his death in 1935. For her part in the feminine lead, reviewers cited Anne Shirley's "delightfully whimsical innocence," a characteristic of many of her roles and a trait for which she was praised in real life. In *Stella Dallas*, from 1937, Anne Shirley probably offered the greatest performance of her career, for which she received an Academy Award nomination. She was Laurel, the gentle-spirited and loyal daughter of Stella, a vulgar harridan who sacrificed a secure future for her beloved child. *Stella Dallas*, with Barbara Stanwyck in the title role, contains many moving and emotional scenes. Although it is basically a "woman's movie," it is now considered a classic of the "romantic film" genre. Other critics said that Miss Shirley's role in *Murder, My Sweet*, opposite Dick Powell, was her best. This 1945 offering was her last film.

Many of the films of Anne Shirley are shown on television now. The following is a listing of the movies in which she appeared before retiring at age 25 after 22 years of acting in the movies.

The films of Dawn O'Day are as follows: 1923, *The Spanish Dancer*; 1924, *The Man Who Fights Alone*; 1924, *The Fast Set*; 1925, *Riders of the Purple Sage*; 1928, *4 Devils*; 1929, *Sins of the Fathers*; 1931, *Gun Smoke*; 1931, *Rich Man's Folly*; 1932, *So Big*; 1932, *Young America*; 1932, *The Purchase Price*; 1933, *The Life of Jimmy Dolan*; 1934, *Finishing School*; 1934, *The Key*.

The films of Anne Shirley are as follows: 1934, *Anne of Green Gables*

1935, *Steamboat Round the Bend*; 1936, *Chatterbox*; 1936, *M'liss*; 1936, *Make Way for a Lady*; 1937, *Meet the Missus*; 1937, *Stella Dallas*; 1938, *Condemned Woman*; 1938, *Law of the Underworld*; 1938, *Mother Carey's Chickens*; 1938, *Girls' School*; 1938, *A Man to Remember*; 1939, *Boy Slaves*; 1939, *Career*; 1940, *Vigil in the Night*; 1940, *Saturday's Children*; 1940, *Anne of Windy Poplars*; 1941, *West Point Widow*; 1941, *Unexpected Uncle*; 1941, *All That Money Can Buy*; 1942, *The Mayor of Forty-Fourth Street*; 1943, *The Powers Girl*; 1943, *Bombardier*; 1944, *Government Girl*; 1944, *Man From Frisco*; 1944, *Music in Manhattan*; 1945, *Murder, My Sweet*.

Doll collectors, especially those of celebrity dolls, seek and prize collectibles such as portraits, "stills" from the movies and film advertising posters. Many unusual and interesting things relating to these dolls also turn up besides the expected coloring books and paper dolls. Of the more unusual collectibles is one such as the Hollywood Dress Patterns. The dresses were not an outright endorsement by the star, but each one featured a photograph of a well-known favorite.

During the time of the manufacture of the most popular composition dolls — the 1930s and the 1940s — almost every consumer product was endorsed by a Hollywood film star and touted by one in magazine advertisements. The advertising data relating to celebrity dolls is also a sought-after addition to the collection.

Dawn Evelyeen Paris who became Dawn O'Day who became Anne Shirley is now married to Charles Lederer [in 1976], the scenarist, film director, producer and writer. Among his many accomplishments, Charles Lederer is the co-author of the fantastically successful musical *Kismet*. Mrs. Lederer till [in 1976] sees her friends from her days as a Hollywood star and continues to maintain her interest in film work. Most of all she enjoys her life at her home in Malibu where she has six cats and the entire Pacific Ocean.

Anne Shirley has no desire to work again in the movies but, because of them and the little *Anne Shirleys* in countless doll collections, she is immortal. □

Illustration 3. *18in (46cm)* Little Ladies; *marked "EffanBee// U.S.A.;" all-composition with mohair wigs and blue sleep eyes; original outfits. They have the same modeling as the marked* Anne Shirley *dolls.*

Illustration 4. *13½in (34cm) and 15½in (39cm) all-original* Honeys; *all hard plastic and in like-new condition with highly styled saran wigs, sleep eyes (blue on the smaller flower girl and brown on the taller bridesmaid); marked only on the backs: "EffanBee."*

INDEX

Other Books by John Axe

Collectible Boy Dolls

Collectible Dolls in National Costume

The Collectible Dionne Quintuplets

Collectible Black Dolls

Collectible Patsy Dolls and Patsy-Types

Collectible Sonja Henie

Tammy and Dolls You Love to Dress

The Encyclopedia of Celebrity Dolls

Effanbee: A Collector's Encyclopedia 1949-1983

Celebrity Doll Price Guide and Annual
(with A. Glenn Mandeville)

The Magic of Merrythought

Kewpies — Dolls & Art of Rose O'Neill and Joseph L. Kallus

Paper Doll Books

Romantic Heroes of Fiction Paper Dolls

Royal Children Paper Dolls: Queen Victoria to Queen Elizabeth II